HIKING SOUTH DAKOTA

HELP US KEEP THIS GUIDE UP TO DATE

Every effort has been made by the author and editors to make this guide as accurate and useful as possible. However, many things can change after a guide is published—trails are rerouted, regulations change, techniques evolve, facilities come under new management, etc.

We appreciate hearing from you concerning your experiences with this guide and how you feel it could be improved and kept up to date. While we may not be able to respond to all comments and suggestions, we'll take them to heart, and we'll also make certain to share them with the author. Please send your comments and suggestions to the following address:

FalconGuides
Reader Response/Editorial Department
Falconeditorial@rowman.com

Thanks for your input, and happy trails!

HIKING SOUTH DAKOTA

A GUIDE TO THE STATE'S GREATEST HIKING ADVENTURES

Marcus Heerdt

FALCON GUIDES

ESSEX, CONNECTICUT

FALCONGUIDES®

An imprint of Globe Pequot, the trade division of The Rowman & Littlefield Publishing Group, Inc.
64 Forbes Blvd., Ste. 200
Lanham, MD 20706
www.rowman.com

Falcon and FalconGuides are registered trademarks and Make Adventure Your Story is a
trademark of The Rowman & Littlefield Publishing Group, Inc.

Distributed by NATIONAL BOOK NETWORK

Copyright © 2024 The Rowman & Littlefield Publishing Group, Inc.
Photos by Marcus Heerdt unless otherwise noted
Additional photos provided by the National Park Service (NPS), Travel South Dakota, Joseph N.
Nicollet Tower and Interpretive Center, Brittany Kahl, Andrew Peschong, Joan F. Carroll, John
Mitchell, Andrea Fountain, Kim Nordby, Frank Thuringer, Erica Knox, Erin Brady, Sharon Koller,
and Marilyn Heerdt
Maps by Melissa Baker and The Rowman & Littlefield Publishing Group, Inc.

British Library Cataloguing in Publication Information available

Library of Congress Cataloging-in-Publication Data
Names: Heerdt, Marcus, 1987– author.
Title: Hiking South Dakota : a guide to the state's greatest hiking
    adventures / Marcus Heerdt.
Description: Essex, Connecticut : FalconGuides, [2024] | Includes
    bibliographical references and index. | Summary: "A guide to 50 hikes to
    mountains, forests, lakes, rivers, waterfalls, plains, and badlands
    formations throughout the state. Hikes are distributed across five
    regions: the Glacial Lakes, Southeast, Missouri River, Badlands, and
    Black Hills"— Provided by publisher.
Identifiers: LCCN 2023027827 (print) | LCCN 2023027828 (ebook) | ISBN
    9781493068616 (paperback) | ISBN 9781493068623 (epub)
Subjects: LCSH: Hiking—South Dakota—Guidebooks. | South
    Dakota--Guidebooks.
Classification: LCC GV199.42.S6 H44 2024 (print) | LCC GV199.42.S6
    (ebook) | DDC 796.5109783—dc23/eng/20230711
LC record available at https://lccn.loc.gov/2023027827
LC ebook record available at https://lccn.loc.gov/2023027828

∞™ The paper used in this publication meets the minimum requirements of American National
Standard for Information Sciences—Permanence of Paper for Printed Library Materials,
ANSI/NISO Z39.48-1992.

CONTENTS

OVERVIEW MAP   viii

ACKNOWLEDGMENTS   ix

MEET YOUR GUIDE   x

WELCOME TO SOUTH DAKOTA   1

BEFORE YOU HIT THE TRAIL   35

MAP LEGEND   39

THE HIKES

Glacial Lakes   40

SICA HOLLOW STATE PARK   42
  1 Trail of the Spirits   43
FORT SISSETON HISTORIC STATE PARK   46
  2 Fort Sisseton Trail System   47
WAUBAY NATIONAL WILDLIFE REFUGE   50
  3 Headquarters Island Trail System   52
HARTFORD BEACH STATE PARK   54
  4 Hartford Beach Trail System   56
OAKWOOD LAKES STATE PARK   58
  5 Oakwood Lakes Trail System   60
LAKE HERMAN STATE PARK   62
  6 Lake Herman Trail System   64

Southeast   65

PALISADES STATE PARK   67
  7 Palisades Trail System   69
BIG SIOUX RECREATION AREA   71
  8 Valley of the Giants Trail   73
  9 Prairie Vista Trail   75
BEAVER CREEK NATURE AREA   77
  10 Homesteader Nature Trail   79
GOOD EARTH STATE PARK   81
  11 Good Earth Trail System   83

NEWTON HILLS STATE PARK   85

12   Woodland Trail   87

UNION GROVE STATE PARK   89

13   Brule Bottom Trail   91

Missouri River   *93*

ADAMS HOMESTEAD AND NATURE PRESERVE   95

14   Adams Homestead Trail System   97

SPIRIT MOUND HISTORIC PRAIRIE   100

15   Spirit Mound Summit Trail   102

LEWIS AND CLARK RECREATION AREA   104

16   Gavins Point Nature Trail   106

17   Chalk Bluffs Loop   108

PEASE CREEK RECREATION AREA   110

18   Pease Creek Trail System   112

FARM ISLAND RECREATION AREA   114

19   Farm Island Trail System   116

LAFRAMBOISE ISLAND NATURE AREA   118

20   LaFramboise Island Trail System   120

OAHE DOWNSTREAM RECREATION AREA   122

21   Cottonwood Path   124

WEST WHITLOCK RECREATION AREA   126

22   Lewis Badger Trail   128

Badlands   *131*

BADLANDS NATIONAL PARK   133

23 Castle-Medicine Root Loop   136

24 Door Trail   138

25 Window Trail   140

26 Notch Trail   141

27   Cliff Shelf Nature Trail   144

28   Saddle Pass Trail   146

Black Hills   *148*

BEAR BUTTE STATE PARK   150

29   Bear Butte Summit Trail   153

SPEARFISH AREA   156

30   Crow Peak   159

31   Roughlock Falls   162

32   Spearfish Falls   165

33   '76 Trail   167

CUSTER STATE PARK 169
  34 Sunday Gulch Trail 172
  35 Lovers' Leap Trail 176
  36 Grace Coolidge Walk-in Fishing Area 180
BLACK ELK RANGE 183
  37 Sylvan Lake to Black Elk Peak 186
  38 Little Devils Tower Trailhead to Black Elk Peak 190
  39 Little Devils Tower Spur Trail 193
  40 Lost Cabin–Black Elk Peak Loop 196
  41 Cathedral Spires Trail 200
  42 Iron Mountain Loop 202
CENTRAL BLACK HILLS–FLUME TRAIL 205
  43 Boulder Hill 207
  44 Spring Creek Loop B 209
WIND CAVE NATIONAL PARK 211
  45 Rankin Ridge Nature Trail 214
  46 Lookout Point–Centennial Trail Loop 216
JEWEL CAVE AREA 220
  47 Roof Trail 223
  48 Hell Canyon Trail 225
MOUNT RUSHMORE 228
  49 Presidential Trail 231
  50 Horsethief Lake to Mount Rushmore 233

The Long Trails of the Black Hills 236

Bonus Hikes at a Glance 240
  Glacial Mounds Trail 240
  Pheasant Run Trail 241
  Shannon Trail to Scenic Overlook 242
  Prairie Falcon Trail 243
  Fossil Exhibit Trail 244
  Mount Roosevelt (Friendship Tower) 245
  Stockade Lake Trail 246
  Elk Mountain Nature Trail 247
  Prairie Vista Nature Trail and Natural Entrance 248
  Cold Brook Canyon Trail 249

APPENDIX A: SUGGESTED EQUIPMENT 250
APPENDIX B: MANAGING AGENCIES 253
APPENDIX C: SELECTED BIBLIOGRAPHY
  AND FURTHER READING 258

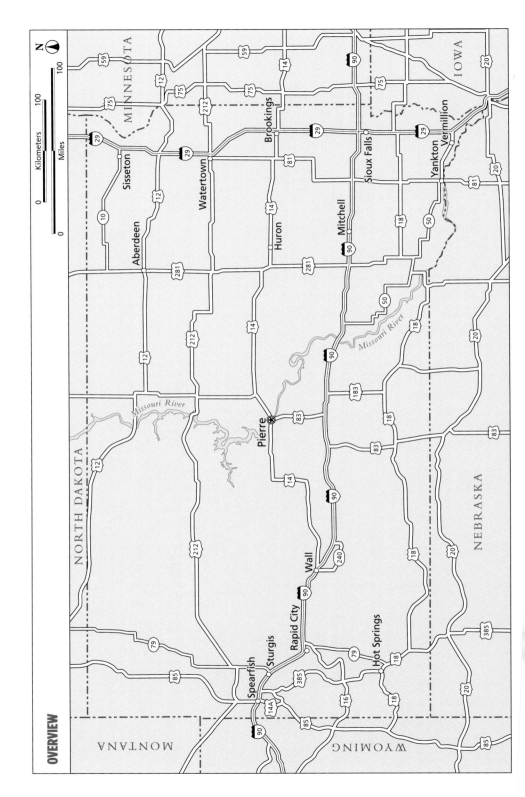

OVERVIEW

ACKNOWLEDGMENTS

Many individuals from the different public lands agencies and other organizations across South Dakota helped with this guidebook. Thank you to everyone who answered my questions and provided great insight. Some of the following individuals have since moved on to different careers or switched agencies, but their job titles are listed as where they were employed at the time I reached out to them.

I would like to thank Sara Erickson, Benjamin Schumacher, and Bradley Block from the various Black Hills National Forest ranger districts; Tom Farrell, Lennie Ramacher, and Marc Ohms from Wind Cave National Park; Aimee M. Murillo of Jewel Cave National Monument; Kobee Stalder of Custer State Park; LaRayne Woster, teacher at St. Joseph's Indian School in Chamberlain; Martin and Lisa Freidel; Sarah Shoop and the staff of the Phoebe Apperson Hearst Library in Lead; the staff of the Hot Springs Public Library; Nick Harrington, South Dakota Game, Fish and Parks communications manager; Shawn Hendricks and Josh Cleveland, Hartford Beach State Park; Becky Graff, Oakwood Lakes State Park; Nicholas Blaske, executive director of the Sisseton Area Chamber of Commerce; Jody Williamson of the Glacial Lakes & Prairies Tourism Association of Northeast South Dakota; John Rasmussen, president of the Heritage Museums of the Coteau des Prairies; Ciara Forest, global media and public relations representative for the South Dakota Department of Tourism; author Paul L. Hedren; Bradley Johnson, Waubay National Wildlife Refuge; John Andrews, managing editor of *South Dakota Magazine*; Andrew Becker, West Whitlock Recreation Area; Ali Jo Tonsfeldt, Fort Sisseton Historic State Park; Ryan Raynor, Farm Island Recreation Area; Caleb Wynia, Newton Hills State Park; Luke Hummel and Shane Bertsch, Lewis and Clark Recreation Area; John Dummer, Big Sioux Recreation Area; Samuel Smolnisky, Custer County Search and Rescue director; Jen Stahl, Good Earth State Park; Dennis H. Knight, W. Carter Johnson, Malia Volke, Kenneth L. Driese, and Donna Anstey, who were all involved in obtaining the necessary permissions to use maps from the book *Ecology of Dakota Landscapes: Past, Present, and Future*; Tim Cowman with the South Dakota Geological Survey; Andrea Fountain; Dr. Ric Dias at Northern State University in Aberdeen; Cassie Vogt, state archaeologist; Dr. Jennifer Fowler; Dr. Hazel Barton; and all the amazing photographers who agreed to collaborate on this project. If I have forgotten anyone, I am truly sorry.

This book would not have been possible without the guidance and support of Mason Gadd, Katherine O'Dell, Emily Vollmer, Maura Cahill, Meredith Dias, Melissa Baker, Karen Weldon, and Lynn Zelem from FalconGuides.

Marcus Heerdt lives and works in the beautiful Black Hills of South Dakota in the southern Hills community of Hot Springs. He has a wandering spirit that has led him to many amazing places. His hiking adventures have taken him to each of the fifty states as well as far-away places such as the Yukon Territory, Spain, Russia, and Kyrgyzstan.

Marcus loves taking pictures and writing stories about his adventures. His work has appeared in books, newspapers, magazines, edited collections, and online publications. Currently, he is an award-winning reporter for the *Fall River County Herald-Star* newspaper in Hot Springs.

In his free time, he enjoys being near water—swimming, kayaking, waterskiing, and fishing. His personal website is www.marcusheerdt.com.

He is the author of *Hiking the Black Hills Country*, 3rd edition, and *Best Easy Day Hikes Black Hills Country*, 2nd edition, by FalconGuides as well as the local history book *Naming Writes: A Series of Stories Written about the Local Places of Today, Named for the People of Yesterday.*

"Marcus—way atop high rock above Sylvan Lake, S.D. August 1991." Photo and caption by Marilyn Heerdt (1925–2019)

INTRODUCTION

WELCOME TO SOUTH DAKOTA

Welcome to The Mount Rushmore State! South Dakota is a great place to get outside and explore new places. From the wooded banks of the Big Sioux River on the eastern border to the peaks of the Black Hills mountain range on the western, South Dakota offers something for everyone.

Mount Rushmore

GEOGRAPHIC REGIONS

South Dakota is oftentimes referred to as "the land of infinite variety," and the descriptions that follow will illustrate how that is true.

This guidebook divides South Dakota into five distinct regions from east to west: Glacial Lakes, Southeast, Missouri River, Badlands, and Black Hills. I chose a mixture of how the South Dakota Department of Tourism splits the state into separate tourism regions (visit its travel website at www.travelsouthdakota.com) as well as how the South Dakota Department of Game, Fish and Parks (https://gfp.sd.gov) sections its state parks geographically.

I have also included notes on history and geology throughout this guidebook.

GLACIAL LAKES

The northeastern section of South Dakota is scattered with glacial lakes, forests, rivers, farmlands, and prairies. Coteau des Prairies (meaning "Hills of the Prairie," also known locally as Buffalo Ridge) is a unique geologic feature of the area. The ridge was formed by glaciation during the last ice age, and early French explorers subsequently gave it its name. The Coteau is a high, grassy plateau that stretches about 200 miles from

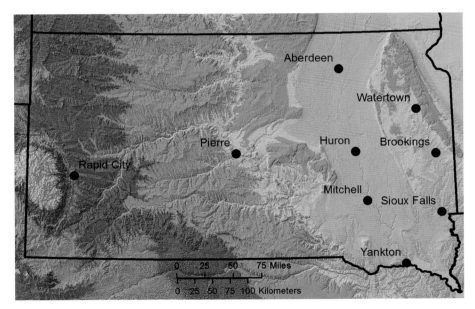

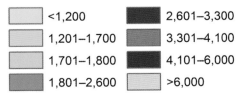

Elevation (feet)

<1,200	2,601–3,300
1,201–1,700	3,301–4,100
1,701–1,800	4,101–6,000
1,801–2,600	>6,000

South Dakota elevation map KENNETH L. DRIESE/*ECOLOGY OF DAKOTA LANDSCAPES* southeastern North Dakota, through eastern South Dakota and southwestern Minnesota, to northwestern Iowa (see elevation map; it is the flatiron-like elevation relief on the east side). Numerous state parks with excellent hiking trails exist in this region, and most can be found near its ridges, lakes, and rivers. The lakes of northeastern South Dakota, a part of the prairie pothole region, were formed in the depressions left by receding glaciers.

Perhaps the most interesting trail in the northeast is the Trail of the Spirits (Hike 1), a designated National Recreation Trail at Sica Hollow State Park.

Visitors to the area can also experience the history of the American West at places such as Fort Sisseton Historic State Park (Hike 2).

No trip to northeast South Dakota is complete without a visit to Nicollet Tower. The tower was built in the early 1990s and is named for Joseph N. Nicollet, a French map-maker who explored the area in the 1830s. The tower is located near the city of Sisseton and sits on a high point of the Coteau. A climb to the top of the tower rewards visitors with commanding views of three states.

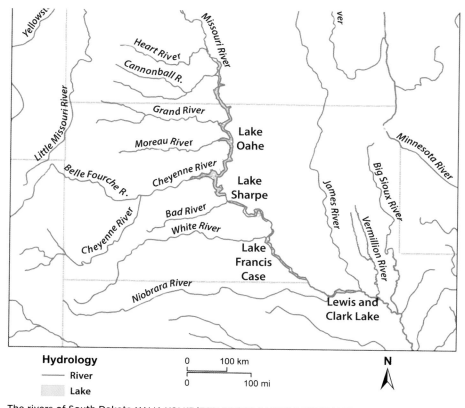

The rivers of South Dakota MALIA VOLKE/*ECOLOGY OF DAKOTA LANDSCAPES*

Joseph N. Nicollet Tower JOSEPH N. NICOLLET TOWER AND INTERPRETIVE CENTER

SOUTHEAST

Southeastern South Dakota is the most populated region of the state, yet some of the state's best hikes are located close to Sioux Falls, the state's largest metro area. When visiting Sioux Falls, make plans to visit Falls Park, a 128-acre park near the downtown area that features a series of cascading waterfalls along the Big Sioux River.

The area is filled with Sioux quartzite rock outcroppings, rivers, forests, lakes, and in the southeast corner, the Missouri River, which forms a portion of the border with neighboring Nebraska.

Palisades State Park (page 67), just northeast of Sioux Falls, is the perfect place to hike or rock climb up the Sioux quartzite formations.

Native American history has been preserved at South Dakota's state parks in the southeast at places such as Good Earth (page 81) and Newton Hills State Parks (page 85).

MISSOURI RIVER

The Missouri River begins near Three Forks, Montana, and flows for more than 2,000 miles before its confluence with the Mississippi River near St. Louis, Missouri. The Missouri River (nicknamed the "Big Muddy") almost cuts South Dakota in two halves as it winds its way through the central portion of the state. Hiking, boating, fishing, birding, and camping opportunities abound in the area. There are four dams along the Missouri River in South Dakota that create four large lakes (from southeast to northwest): Gavins Point Dam (Lewis and Clark Lake), Fort Randall Dam (Lake Francis Case), Big Bend Dam (Lake Sharpe), and Oahe Dam (Lake Oahe).

Morning at Falls Park FRANK THURINGER

Pierre (pronounced "peer"), South Dakota's capital city, is located along the Missouri River and is close to state parks with hiking and biking trails.

A portion of Farm Island Recreation Area (page 114) is located on an island in the Missouri River with almost 5 miles of trails that lead hikers to abandoned Civilian Conservation Corps (CCC) ruins.

Spirit Mound Historic Prairie (page 100) is an interesting geological, historical, and cultural site located near the Missouri River. Traditional Native American stories told of the "hill of little people" and "place of the Devils." In 1804, Meriwether Lewis and William Clark hiked to the top of the hill. The expedition did not report seeing any spirits, but did observe hundreds of bison (buffalo) roaming on the surrounding prairie.

If driving along I-90 across the state, make sure to stop at the Chamberlain rest area to view the impressive 50-foot Dignity statue, located on a bluff overlooking the Missouri River. The Dignity statue was installed at the site in 2016 and was created to honor the culture of the state's Native American people.

For off-trail wandering near the Missouri River, head to Fort Pierre National Grassland, which is located west of the river, south of the city of Fort Pierre, and north of I-90.

The Missouri River hikes in this guidebook follow the river from southeast to northwest.

Dignity statue JOHN MITCHELL

The many different colors of South Dakota's Badlands

BADLANDS

Badlands National Park is one of the most extraordinary areas of the state if not the entire region. Its topography was formed over millions of years from a mixture of sediment runoff from the Black Hills and volcanic ash from present-day Colorado. It is also home to the largest mixed-grass prairie in the United States as well as a large bison herd. Unique hiking opportunities abound within the park.

The Notch Trail (Hike 26) leads hikers through a canyon and then up a fifty-six-rung rope ladder to the rim of the canyon. The trail ends at the top of a cliff and offers a commanding overlook of the valley below.

The Castle-Medicine Root Loop (Hike 23) combines the Castle Trail and the Medicine Root Trail to make a 6.8-mile loop through badlands formations, grassy plateaus, and geologic rock creations known as "toadstools."

Badlands National Park offers two fully accessible trails: the Window Trail (Hike 25) and the Fossil Exhibit Trail (see Bonus Hikes). The former leads visitors to a natural "window" that offers views of a deep canyon. The latter is a short loop trail with exhibits of fossils that have been found in the area, such as alligators and three-toed horses.

Additionally, Badlands National Park is surrounded by Buffalo Gap National Grassland, which offers even more opportunities to head out on your own and explore the area by foot or on horseback. Stop in to the National Grasslands Visitor Center in the town of Wall to learn more.

Also while in the area, plan to visit the nearby Minuteman Missile National Historic Site to learn about the fascinating Cold War history when thousands of missiles were strategically placed throughout the Great Plains.

The National Grasslands Visitor Center in Wall

BLACK HILLS

The Black Hills are the gem of the northern Great Plains. This rugged mountain range in the western part of the state is home to what has long been referred to as the highest peak east of the main chain of the Rocky Mountains—Black Elk Peak—which is formed of granite that is approximately 1.7 to 2.5 billion years old. At an elevation of 7,242 feet, views of four states can be obtained by hiking to the top (Hikes 37, 38, and 40).

Wind Cave National Park is located in the southern Black Hills and has more than 30 miles of surface hiking trails. Many family-friendly hikes exist in the park, with one of the most popular being the Rankin Ridge Nature Trail (Hike 45). The trail leads visitors to an old fire tower at the top of the ridge and offers wonderful views of the park.

Hiking, snowshoeing, cross-country skiing, swimming, fishing, and many more outdoor opportunities exist within the Black Hills. This guidebook features hikes throughout the different areas of the Black Hills: Bear Butte State Park, Spearfish Area, Custer State Park, Black Elk Range, Central Black Hills–Flume Trail, Wind Cave National Park, Jewel Cave Area, and Mount Rushmore.

The Black Hills have two long trails (page 148), each more than 100 miles total: The Centennial Trail (hiking trail) and the George S. Mickelson Trail (predominantly a bike trail). Both trails run north–south through the heart of the Hills. For complete hike descriptions of these trails, see *Hiking the Black Hills Country*, also by FalconGuides.

Be aware that two of the Hills' most popular scenic drives, the Iron Mountain Road and the Needles Highway, contain a series of tunnels, so it is important to know your vehicle's height and width. Maps with the tunnel locations and their size restrictions are available at visitor centers in the Black Hills (such as a local chamber of commerce) and are listed on official Custer State Park maps and publications. During winter portions of the Needles Highway close for the season, and the Iron Mountain Road often closes due to weather conditions.

Sunset in the central core of the Black Hills

Forest Recreation Management, an official partner of Black Hills National Forest, operates many of the campgrounds, boat ramps, day-use areas, and picnic grounds within the forest. Select areas require a day-use fee. Annual passes are also available for purchase. Visit www.fs.usda.gov/bhnf to learn more.

SHOUT-OUT TO NORTHWEST SOUTH DAKOTA
Off-trail wandering opportunities exist in the northwest corner of the state at places such as the Custer Gallatin National Forest and Grand River National Grassland.

Bighorn sheep

Bald eagle ERICA KNOX

American mink ERIN BRADY

Mountain goat

Plains bison

Black-footed ferret NATIONAL PARK SERVICE

Burrowing owl SHARON KOLLER

Elk NATIONAL PARK SERVICE

Mountain lion tracks

Coyote

Pheasant TRAVEL SOUTH DAKOTA

Pronghorn ERIN BRADY

Red-breasted nuthatch

Mule deer

Prairie dog babies

HISTORY

This book is intended to support your explorations. Readers will come away with a deeper knowledge of the area and the opportunity to connect more closely and experience more fully the wonders these lands offer. FalconGuides respectfully acknowledges that this book covers the traditional land of Native peoples.

Early Native Peoples

Paleo-Indians inhabited what is now present-day South Dakota as early as 12,000 BCE. These Paleo-Indians lived in small family groups and were primarily nomadic big-game hunters and foragers. After the Paleo-Indians, as early as 6000 BCE, Archaic foragers hunted animals such as bison and foraged for food. Next, from 1000 BCE to 800 CE, Woodland villagers were the dominant inhabitants of the region, mostly along the Missouri and Big Sioux Rivers. (For more information about the Woodland culture, refer to the Oakwood Lakes (page 58) and Newton Hills (page 85) State Parks chapters of this guidebook.) Middle Missouri villagers then lived in sustained settlements near the Missouri River from 800 CE to 1600 CE. These sedentary villagers grew crops such as squash, beans, corn, and sunflowers. Around 1300 CE, the Arikaras (also known as the Ree) moved into the area and settled along the Missouri River in earthen lodges. Their economy thrived on crop surpluses that they could trade to neighboring tribes. The Arikara would eventually move north to present-day North Dakota after the territorial expansion of the Sioux.

The Sioux

The Sioux (*Oceti Sakowin*: "Seven Council Fires"), a nation comprising seven tribes or nations, began to move west from the Mississippi River valley in the 1700s and eventually became the dominant Native nation in what is now South Dakota. The Dakota Sioux settled mostly in the eastern areas of the state, the Nakota Sioux settled mostly in the middle, and the Lakota Sioux (which is the largest tribe) settled mostly in the west.

Early Euro-American Explorers

Spanish, French, and British explorers traversed the lands and waterways of the North American interior in the 1600s, 1700s, and 1800s. The fur trade became an important economic industry in what is now South Dakota, with numerous fur trading posts established along the region's rivers.

After the Louisiana Purchase in 1803, which included the majority of present-day South Dakota, President Thomas Jefferson sent Meriwether Lewis and William Clark to explore the newly acquired lands and beyond. Hoping to find an all-water route from the nation's interior to the Pacific Ocean, the Lewis and Clark Expedition departed the St. Louis, Missouri, area in 1804 and traveled up the Missouri River through today's South Dakota. The Corps of Discovery eventually did reach the Pacific (but did not discover a waterway connecting the Missouri to the ocean), and in 1806, voyaged back down the Missouri River through South Dakota on their way back to St. Louis.

The Lakota and the Black Hills

The Lakota Sioux (also known as the Teton Sioux), comprised of seven distinct bands—Brule, Oglala, Two Kettle(s), Sans Arc, Miniconjou, Hunkpapa, and Blackfeet—became the most powerful tribe on the northern Great Plains by the 1800s. Settling into what is now western South Dakota and beyond, the Lakotas forced out other Plains tribes who hunted in the Black Hills region, including the Crows, Poncas, Plains Apaches, Kiowas, Kiowa-Apaches, Cheyennes, and Arapahos. The Black Hills not only became sacred to the Lakotas, but the small mountain range also was (and is) at the center of their universe.

The US government guaranteed what is now present-day western South Dakota, including the Black Hills, to the Sioux Nation in the 1868 Fort Laramie Treaty. However, with orders to find a location for a new fort and investigate rumors of gold, Lieutenant Colonel George A. Custer led an expedition into the Black Hills in 1874. The expedition confirmed the existence of gold in the Black Hills and a gold rush followed, bringing thousands of prospectors to the area. Following the Great Sioux War, also known as the Black Hills War, of 1876 and 1877, the US government took back the Black Hills from the Sioux in 1877 and confined them to smaller reservations.

Custer's Fate

Two years after his expedition into the Black Hills, Custer's regiment of the 7th US Cavalry along with their Arikara and Crow scouts were defeated by members of the Lakota, Northern Cheyenne, and Arapaho Nations at the Battle of the Little Bighorn (also known as the Battle of the Greasy Grass) in present-day southeastern Montana. Custer was killed in the action.

Statehood

The Territory of Dakota was created in 1861 and included the most-northern lands that had been acquired by the United States in the Louisiana Purchase of 1803. With the population increasing in the following decades after the purchase, the territory was officially split into two new states on November 2, 1889: North Dakota and South Dakota, the 39th and 40th states admitted to the Union.

Mining, Ranching, and Farming

The Black Hills gold rush of the 1870s brought thousands of gold-seekers to the Black Hills. Deposits of gold were discovered throughout the Hills. Perhaps the most well-known gold rush town of the Black Hills is Deadwood, which is also the location where American West folk hero James Butler "Wild Bill" Hickok was killed in 1876 while playing cards. The city of Lead (pronounced "leed") is home to the Homestake Mine, which operated for 125 years until its closing in 2002 and was the largest gold mine in North America. Visitors to Lead can still see the massive "open cut" and learn about the mine at the Sanford Lab Homestake Visitor Center.

Homesteaders also poured into the area. Free land offered by the Homestead Act of 1862 attracted settlers of all kinds to present-day South Dakota, not only from across the United States but also the world. Cattle ranching took hold in the western areas of the state, while farming dominated the eastern.

Homestake Mine open cut in Lead

South Dakota Today

Pierre is the state capital of South Dakota and is located in the central part of the state along the Missouri River. The river traverses through the middle of the state, and lands to the east of the river are locally referred to as "East River," with lands to the west known as "West River." The majority of East River lands have been sculpted by glaciers, while West River has unglaciated terrain.

Among the fifty states, South Dakota is ranked 17th in total land area and is among the smallest states in regards to population. The state's economy relies heavily on agriculture, manufacturing, tourism, and the service industry. Farmland is abundant east of the Missouri, while ranchland dominates the landscape of the western region outside the Black Hills.

When hiking during the spring in the Black Hills, be on the lookout for the American pasqueflower, the state's official flower. When traveling around the state, you will most likely see the state's official bird, the ring-necked pheasant, hanging out on the prairies.

South Dakota capitol building in Pierre TRAVEL SOUTH DAKOTA

South Dakota Tribes

Currently, nine federally recognized Native American tribes reside in South Dakota:

- Cheyenne River Sioux
- Crow Creek Sioux
- Flandreau Santee Sioux
- Lower Brule Sioux
- Oglala Sioux
- Rosebud Sioux
- Sisseton-Wahpeton Oyate
- Standing Rock Sioux
- Yankton Sioux

Native Americans' Day

Native Americans' Day in South Dakota is celebrated on the second Monday in October.

HELPFUL INFORMATION

Other important information to support your adventures in South Dakota.

Clothing and Equipment

Here are a few suggestions for a hiker's attire: First, dress in layers. The layer closest to your skin should be a light, inner layer made of material that will wick away moisture from the skin. Next should be a warmer layer that can be removed if necessary. Over that, wear an outside layer that is wind- and/or rainproof. This layering system permits you to regulate your temperature easier by putting on or peeling off layers as weather and exertion dictate. Along with these basics, bring along a good rain poncho or coat as part of your standard hiking equipment. Rain, snow, sleet, and hailstorms can oftentimes be frequent and unpredictable.

Boots or shoes are a matter of personal preference but, regardless of style and weight, should be sturdy and supportive. Many people wear good leather boots for serious hiking, while others prefer lightweight boots with breathable, water-resistant fabrics; visit a good outfitter or outdoor recreation store and try on several styles before finally deciding.

Planning the Hike

Hiking should be fun, even if you hike just for the benefits of physical fitness. To keep it that way, plan hikes that are within your physical ability. Do not attempt long trails or backpacking segments that are more than you can safely accomplish in daylight. Hiking after dark is not only uncomfortable but also dangerous, especially if you are not familiar with the topography and trail conditions. Familiarize yourself with the terrain, and study maps before you depart.

Always leave an itinerary with someone before you leave. This should include where you will be hiking, where you will park, your estimated time for completing the trip, and whom to contact if necessary. This will lead help to you if by unlucky chance you have a trail accident, or if there is some other kind of emergency.

No hike, whether a day hike or a weeklong backpack trip, should begin without the basic essentials of a first-aid kit and simple survival items. The contents of a first-aid kit will depend on each hiker's needs and concerns. For a day hike, it should contain at least adhesive bandages, gauze or gauze compresses, adhesive tape, an elastic wraparound bandage, aspirin or other pain relievers, antibacterial ointment, moleskin, and scissors (or a pocketknife with scissors). A first-aid kit for overnight hikes should contain these same things as well as an antihistamine for allergic responses, hydrocortisone cream, a mild laxative, something to combat diarrhea, and other personal items.

Survival kits can and should be efficient. Carry a compact space blanket or large garbage bag, a whistle, waterproof matches or a reliable cigarette lighter, a compass, a high-energy food bar, 10 or 20 feet of light nylon rope, and a small flashlight. Keep the kit with you at all times, especially when on side trips away from your backpack or campsite.

And do not forget to bring enough water. Do not depend on trying to find potable water at trailheads or along the route. Water in streams and lakes can look refreshing but may contain a microorganism called giardia, which causes severe diarrhea and dehydration in humans. The microorganism is spread through the feces of wild mammals—especially beavers. Any surface water supply is a potential source of this organism, and hikers who drink from lakes and streams take the risk of contracting the painful symptoms associated with this microbe. Water can be rendered safe by boiling it for at least 5 minutes or by passing it through a filter system.

Severe Weather Tips

Always stay tuned to local radio or television stations, and also pay attention to your cell phone for any and all severe weather alerts.

Seek shelter immediately in the nearest sturdy building if a tornado warning is issued.

Thunderstorms that are capable of producing torrential rain, sharp lightning, hail, and tornadoes can occur anywhere within the state of South Dakota, predominantly in the spring and summer.

If caught in a lightning storm, seek shelter away from open ground or exposed ridges. Even dropping a few yards off a ridgetop will reduce your risk. In a forest, stay away from single tall trees; look for a cluster of smaller trees instead. Avoid gullies or small basins with water in the bottom, and find a low spot free of standing water. Stay out of shallow caves, crevasses, or overhangs. Ground discharges may leap across the openings. Dry, deep caves offer better protection, but do not touch the walls.

Whether you are in open country or in a shelter during a lightning storm, assume a low crouch with only your feet touching the ground. Put a sleeping pad or pack (make sure it does not have a metal frame or metal components) beneath your feet for added insulation against shock. Do not huddle together; members of a group should stay at least 30 feet apart. Then, if someone is hit, the others can give first aid. In a tent, get in a crouch position in your sleeping bag and keep your feet on a sleeping pad.

Watch for signs of an imminent lightning strike: hair standing on end; an itchy feeling one hiker described as "bugs crawling all over your skin"; an acrid, "hot metal" smell; and buzzing or crackling noises in the air. Tuck into a crouch immediately if any of these signs are present.

Hypothermia can be a risk in the Black Hills, even in summer, since there are times when the factors contributing to bodily heat loss are present. Cold rains frequently drench the mountains, and it often hails and even snows. Temperatures need not be below freezing for hypothermia to be a threat. Most cases occur when temperatures range between 30 and 50°F, often coupled with windy and wet conditions. Shivering marks the first stage. In advanced stages, shivering stops, but only because the body is too weak to keep it up. This stage may be accompanied by slurred speech, clumsiness, and impaired judgment.

At the first sign of hypothermia, stop and change clothes: Get the victim out of their wet stuff. Feed conscious victims something warm and sweet, such as hot chocolate. Because acute hypothermia can lead to death, seek medical help.

Wildlife

Nature runs wild in South Dakota. The state is home to animals such as bison (buffalo), white-tailed and mule deer, pronghorn (antelope), prairie dogs, mountain goats, bighorn sheep, elk, coyotes, bobcats, and mountain lions. Birders will also enjoy South Dakota, as the state is home to a wide variety of bird species. The South Dakota Department of Game, Fish and Parks provides birding trail brochures for the different regions of the state. Visit https://gfp.sd.gov for more information.

Hundreds of mountain lions and bobcats make South Dakota their home. Mountain lions can be found in sparsely populated areas from the Black Hills to the Missouri River. Lion attacks are rare—in truth, you will be fortunate to catch even a brief glimpse of one of these creatures. If you encounter a lion, remain calm. Back away slowly, taking care to make yourself seem as large as possible, yell and shout, but do not run.

A more likely animal encounter in the Black Hills and Badlands is with bison. Wandering bison often are encountered by hikers at Badlands National Park, Custer State Park, and Wind Cave National Park. Always be aware of the possibility of such encounters. If you do meet up with bison, do not panic. Quietly move away. Remember, if a bison alters its behavior in any way, you are too close. Never approach bison. Bison can run at speeds of 30 to 45 miles per hour. Inquire directly with the public land agencies that manage bison herds to learn more about bison safety and safe distance recommendations.

Additionally, lone black bears, moose, and wolves have been sighted wandering through the Black Hills in recent years; however, the chances of a hiker encountering one of these animals remains low.

People sometimes ask: "What is the difference between a bison and a buffalo?" Well . . . in South Dakota, we have the plains bison. North America has two species of bison: the plains bison and the wood bison. Wood bison are larger than plains bison and live in places like Alaska and Yukon Territory. Across the ocean, there is also a European bison that looks markedly different from those found in North America. Although the term "buffalo" is widely used in North America to refer to plains and wood bison, "true buffalo," such as a water buffalo, are found naturally in parts of Asia and Africa.

Never approach bison and remember to keep your distance from them

In the winter I often snowshoe in the remote backcountry areas of the Black Hills. I am not sure if everyone has a "sixth sense," or sense of intuitive awareness, but I know when I am being watched by someone or some*thing*. It is that weird, unsettling, eerie feeling that shoots across the back of your head and neck area, and your senses perk up, your sight and hearing becoming sharp.

When this occurs, I immediately stop, hold my breath, take off my winter hat, and slowly survey the entire 360-degree area around me. Sometimes I see a curious mule deer peeking out at me from behind a tree. Sometimes it is an elk. But other times I hear the growl of a "big kitty" or catch a glimpse of their shadow gracefully skirting across the bright white snow.

I have never had a negative encounter with a mountain lion. They generally do not want to see you as much as you do not want to come across them. The nearest I have ever been to one (as far as I know) was in the Black Elk Wilderness. I do not know if I woke it up or if it was waiting and hoping that I would veer off in another direction. Or perhaps I was being hunted. Whatever the case, I sensed something but did not see anything. I continued hiking along the trail when it suddenly jumped down from a tree, growled, and ran off. It was probably only 10 yards away.

My favorite bobcat story is the time I was driving in the southern Black Hills and noticed up ahead that something was crossing the road. As I got closer, I saw that it was a bobcat. It stopped in the middle of the road, slowly turned its head at me, and gave me a look like "Grumpy Cat" that was saying: "Are you seriously going to make me walk faster across this road?"

Male house finch

Ticks

Contracting diseases associated with ticks is a distinct possibility. Ticks can appear any time of year if the temperature is above 50°F, even in January and February. If they attach to the skin, they begin to feed.

Lyme disease, Rocky Mountain spotted fever, or human granulocytic ehrlichia infection may result. General symptoms of these diseases include fever with shaking chills and severe muscle pain. Lyme disease also may produce a rash at the site of the tick bite.

The best way to prevent tickborne disease is to prevent ticks from latching onto the skin. Wear long pants and tuck them into boots or bind the bottoms with a rubber band. Consider using a repellent containing DEET, which you should apply to skin and clothing. After a hike, conduct a tick search of your body and clothing.

To remove a loose tick, flick it off with a fingernail. If the tick is firmly embedded, use tweezers to pinch a small area around the tick's mouth and pull it out. Try not to squeeze the tick's body, since this increases the risk of infection. Finally, clean the site with an antiseptic.

The author snowshoeing in the Black Hills ANDREA FOUNTAIN

Mosquitoes

Wearing insect repellent is recommended while hiking in South Dakota. Mosquitoes can carry West Nile virus, an illness that is potentially life-threatening for infected humans.

Snakes

South Dakota is home to a variety of snakes such as prairie rattlesnakes, garter snakes, and smooth green snakes. Prairie rattlesnakes, the only venomous snake in the state, are common in South Dakota west of the Missouri River. If you have never heard a rattlesnake rattle, do not worry: You will recognize it—the sound is unmistakable. Although death from a rattlesnake bite is rare, it *has* happened. Snake venom is relatively slow acting, allowing victims a chance to acquire medical attention.

Learning to avoid snakes and their bites is relatively simple: Watch where you step or sit down to rest. Wear high leather boots and long pants in snake habitat. Avoid hiking at night. Snakes usually hole up by day, then bask on sun-warmed rocks or sand when temperatures cool in the evening. Snakes generally hunt at night, too, so it is best to sleep in tents with sewn-in floors and zippered doors.

Poison Ivy

Hikers easily can learn to identify poison ivy and avoid plants that have shiny foliage consisting of three leaves. Remember the saying: "Leaves of three, let it be." In fall the plant is particularly deceptive, since its leaves turn a beautiful orange and red, and the plant produces a white berry somewhat similar to a snowberry.

If you suspect you have rubbed against poison ivy, wash the area immediately with water from a canteen or a nearby stream. Washing within the first 10 minutes can often prevent irritation. Ideally, you should place suspect clothing in a plastic bag until it can be thoroughly washed either in a stream or (best) by machine. If a rash appears, apply calamine lotion. Persistent rashes may require something stronger, such as a cream containing cortisone.

Trail Etiquette

"Pack it in, pack it out" should be the working motto of every hiker. This is true for short day hikes as much as for wilderness backpack trips.

Many trails are "multiple use," which means that hikers will share the trail with mountain bikers and horseback riders. Trail etiquette requires that bikers yield to hikers and that bikers and hikers yield to stock and riders. If stock is encountered on the trail, hikers should move to the side of the trail to let the stock pass. Horses are sometimes spooked by sudden, unforeseen encounters, so make your presence known.

Trail etiquette also confers the responsibility to care for the environment and respect the rights of others. Check with each individual public land agency for its unique restrictions and regulations. Additionally, always remain respectful of private property.

A Note on Photography

In regards to photography, I wanted *Hiking South Dakota* to be a group effort. I felt that the guidebook should feature photographers from around the state, not just me. Our state deserves it. South Dakota has some amazing photographers, and their work is included throughout this book. Thank you to all who submitted their photos to this project.

Hike Selection

Narrowing down South Dakota's hiking trails to fifty was not an easy task, but I feel that the final selection fairly distributes the hikes across the different geographic regions of the state.

The trails included in this guidebook are all well marked, legal, and managed by a federal, state, or local public agency. This was done on purpose. "Social" trails or "user-submitted" hikes that can oftentimes cross private property are not in this guidebook.

Cell Service

Cell service can be spotty in South Dakota. Plan on not having reliable cell phone service during hikes throughout much of the Badlands and Black Hills. In many of these areas, cell service is nonexistent to begin with. My suggestion will always be to put away your cell phone or turn it on airplane mode and enjoy the beauty of nature with limited distractions.

However, if cell service is necessary, the following is a list of public land agencies included in this guidebook that report that "most" cell phones work on either all or portions of their trails:

- Fort Sisseton Historic State Park
- Hartford Beach State Park
- Oakwood Lakes State Park
- Lake Herman State Park
- Pickerel Lake Recreation Area
- Big Sioux Recreation Area
- Beaver Creek Nature Area
- Union Grove State Park
- Adams Homestead and Nature Preserve
- Spirit Mound Historic Prairie
- Lewis and Clark Recreation Area
- Pease Creek Recreation Area
- Farm Island Recreation Area
- LaFramboise Island Nature Area
- Snake Creek Recreation Area
- Indian Creek Recreation Area
- Bear Butte State Park
- Mount Rushmore National Memorial

Time Zones

South Dakota spans two time zones: Central Time and Mountain Time. Although not precisely split in two, the majority of the eastern side of the state is in the Central Time Zone while the western half is in the Mountain Time Zone. Mountain Time is one hour behind Central Time, or vice versa, Central Time is one hour ahead of Mountain Time. For example, if it is 10 a.m. in Sioux Falls, it is 9 a.m. in Rapid City.

Area Code

South Dakota has one area code: 605. Sometimes you will see advertisements where the phone number only has seven digits (xxx-xxxx). In that case, just know that the first three digits will be 605-xxx-xxxx.

National Park Service (NPS) sites in South Dakota

Badlands National Park

Lewis and Clark National Historic Trail

Cross-country skiing in the Black Hills TRAVEL SOUTH DAKOTA

Before You Hit the Trail
The following explains some of the basic information found in each hike description.

Hike Overview
This provides a brief description of each hike, often listing some of its highlights.

Start
This is a short summary of the starting location for the hike.

Elevation Gain
The two numbers listed are the highest and lowest points reached on the hike. Sometimes the trailhead lies at the lowest point and the end lies at the highest point. Some of the hikes have several ups and downs along the way, requiring more elevation gain and effort than the high and low numbers indicate. At high elevations, lower atmospheric pressure creates "thin air" that requires higher breathing rates and more effort to pull enough oxygen into the lungs. It is important to know your own strengths and limitations.

Distance
Distances in this book refer to the total miles of an out and back, loop, lollipop, figure eight, or entire trail system. Trail lengths have been calculated as closely as possible using a handheld GPS unit and two GPS watches along with official government topographic maps. However, the different sources do not always agree. All distances were rounded to the nearest tenth (with a few exceptions), and any variations of GPS mileages were averaged or checked against official USGS maps.

Difficulty
Assessing a hike's difficulty is very subjective. The elevation, elevation change, and length all play a role, as do trail conditions, weather, and the hiker's physical condition. The trails in this guidebook are rated as easy, moderate, or strenuous.

In specific regards to the Black Hills, many visitors to western South Dakota expect the area to be just "hills," therefore making hiking relatively easy. This assumption is incorrect. The Black Hills are mountains, and hikers may encounter difficult elevation gains. For example, one of the most popular trails in the area, Sylvan Lake to Black Elk Peak, has a total elevation gain of more than 1,400 feet.

Hiking Time

The approximate hiking time is a rough estimate of the time in which the average hiker will be able to complete the hike. Very fit, fast-moving hikers will be able to complete it in less time. Slow-moving hikers or those preoccupied with activities such as photography may take longer. Most people can hike at 2 to 3 miles per hour. For longer hikes with more elevation changes, estimations are closer to 2 miles per hour. Rough trails, carrying a heavy backpack, or particularly big elevation changes are also factors.

Seasons

The season specified for a hike is the optimum or ideal season. The weather in South Dakota varies greatly. In the eastern portion of the state, summers are hot and humid, whereas summers in the west are normally hot and dry. Fall mornings and evenings are cool and crisp. Winters can be harsh and unforgiving. Spring can be very wet and muddy. On average, June is usually the wettest month in South Dakota.

Snow is possible in the Black Hills every month of the year. On average, the northern Hills receive more snowfall during the winter months than southern areas. Some trails may have ice late into spring.

Always check local weather conditions and forecasts before heading out on a trail. This guidebook is written mostly for use during the warm months.

Severe storm moving into Custer State Park in the Black Hills

Fees and Permits

This includes information about fees and permits needed to access hiking trails within the different public land agencies.

Trail Contact

The trail contact category lists the name, address, phone number, and website of the managing agency for the lands through which the trail passes. Call, write, or check the website for current information about the hike.

Dog-Friendly

This tells you if dogs are allowed on the trail or not. Generally, dogs need to be leashed where allowed. Please be courteous and pick up after your dog. At most South Dakota state parks (except Bear Butte, where dogs are not allowed on the trail), dogs must be on a leash or under immediate control. Also check https://gfp.sd.gov/parks/ for current pet restrictions within state nature areas. Dogs are also prohibited in most areas managed by the National Park Service (NPS).

I know people love their dogs, but if dogs are not allowed on the trail, then dogs are not allowed on the trail. I have seen hikers with their dogs walk directly past "No Dogs" signs at trailheads and continue on the trail. Please be respectful of the land and the public land agencies that manage it.

Trail Surface/Conditions

This describes the material that makes up the trail and setting. Examples include dirt path, forested trail, gravel road, etc.

Land Status

The land status simply tells which agency, usually federal or state, manages the land in which the trail lies.

Nearest Town(s)

The nearest town is the closest city or town to the hike's trailhead that has at least minimal visitor services. The listed town will usually have gas, food, and possibly lodging available. In small towns and villages, the hours these services are available may be limited.

Other Trail Users

This describes the other users that you might encounter on the hike. Mountain bikers and horseback riders are the most common.

Trailhead Amenities

This describes available amenities at each trailhead. The most common amenities at trailheads are vault toilets and picnic tables. Amenities may only be offered seasonally and can change over time.

Maximum Grade

This provides the percent grade of the steepest section of the trail and its length.

Maps

The maps included in this guide are as accurate and current as possible. Using these maps in conjunction with the hike description and the additional maps listed will add value to the hike.

Black Hills National Forest publishes a map of the entire forest (for purchase) that includes many of the trails listed in this guidebook. This is referred to as the "Black Hills National Forest Map." The US Forest Service also distributes free individual trail brochures (e.g., Flume Trail No. 50). These can be obtained at national forest district offices (see Appendix B for locations). National Geographic/Trails Illustrated publishes three maps (for purchase) for western South Dakota: *Black Hills North* (Map No. 751), *Black Hills South* (Map No. 238), and *Badlands National Park* (Map No. 239).

Most of the National Park Service areas have maps or brochures showing the trails. Badlands National Park, Wind Cave National Park, Mount Rushmore National Memorial, and Jewel Cave National Monument have brochures available.

Similarly, South Dakota's state parks and recreation areas also offer trail maps for visitors. These maps are normally available at state park entrance stations, at the trailhead, and/or online at https://gfp.sd.gov/parks/. Throughout the guidebook, these maps are simply referred to as "State park map."

Finding the Trailhead

This section provides detailed directions to the trailhead as well as the GPS coordinates at the trailhead. The starting point is usually the nearest city, a park visitor center, or some other major landmark followed by directions on how to get to the trailhead. Be sure to keep an eye open for the specific signs, junctions, and landmarks mentioned in the directions, not just the mileages. The map services available on cell phone GPS systems are often inaccurate or nonexistent in remote areas, so use them with care. In addition, many require decent cell service to work, further lessening their value. Cell phone coverage in the Black Hills and Badlands is nonexistent in many areas. Using a good map is recommended.

Most of the hikes in this guide have trailheads that can be reached with the average vehicle. Except in wet or snowy weather, only a very few may require four-wheel drive. Rain or snow can temporarily make some roads impassable, and many roads close in winter. Before venturing onto unimproved dirt roads, you should check with local entities about current road conditions (South Dakota 511 is a good resource). On less-raveled back roads, you should carry basic emergency equipment such as a shovel, chains, water, a spare tire, a jack, blankets, and extra food and clothing. Make sure that your vehicle is in good operating condition with a full tank of gas. Try not to leave valuables in your car; if you must, lock them out of sight in the trunk.

The Hike

This section provides the trail user an accurate description of each hike, including what will be encountered along the trail and other useful information. It is strongly suggested that you read the hike description before setting out on the trail.

Miles and Directions

To help you stay on course, a detailed route finder sets forth mileages between significant landmarks along the trail. Again, it is strongly suggested that you read the hike description along with the miles and directions before setting out on the trail.

MAP LEGEND

Municipal

≡⃝29≡ Freeway/Interstate Highway

≡⃝281≡ US Highway

≡⃝79≡ State Road

≡⃞222≡ County/Paved/Improved Road

= = = = Unimproved Road

= = = = Unpaved Road

--- --- --- State Boundary

Trails

------ Featured Trail

------ Trail

Water Features

Body of Water

Marsh/Swamp

River/Creek

Waterfall

Land Management

National Park

National Monument/
Wilderness/Preserve

State Park

Symbols

▲ Backcountry Campsite

||||| Boardwalk

⌣ Bridge

■ Building/Point of Interest

▲ Campground

⊛ Capital

† Cemetery

— Dam

▲ Mountain/Peak

Mount Rushmore

🅿 Parking

Picnic Area

Restroom

Scenic View/Overlook

Tower

○ Towns and Cities

① Trailhead

Visitor/Information Center

Water

GLACIAL LAKES

Waubay National Wildlife Refuge TRAVEL SOUTH DAKOTA

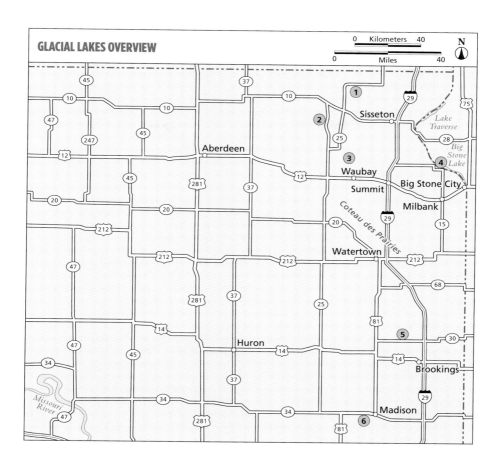

SICA HOLLOW STATE PARK

Located on the northeastern slope of the Coteau des Prairies, Sica (pronounced "she-cha") Hollow State Park is one of the most scenic areas in South Dakota. The park is approximately 20 minutes northwest of the city of Sisseton, which is located just off I-29. The entire park was named a National Natural Landmark in 1967. In 1971 the Trail of the Spirits, the park's interpretive self-guided trail, was designated a National Recreation Trail. In addition to the Trail of the Spirits, the park has about 8 miles of marked horseback riding trails that can also be used by hikers, bikers, and cross-country skiers.

Autumn is a great time to visit Sica Hollow State Park KIM NORDBY

1 TRAIL OF THE SPIRITS

An interpretive trail that explores a scenic area along the Coteau des Prairies in northeastern South Dakota. Native American legends about this area gave the hollow its name, as "sica" translates to "bad."

Start: At the trailhead parking lot in the park's day-use area
Elevation gain: 1,518 to 1,614 feet
Distance: 0.8-mile loop, with shorter options
Difficulty: Easy
Hiking time: 30 minutes to 1 hour
Seasons: Best late spring through fall
Fees and permits: Park entrance fee
Trail contact: Sica Hollow State Park, 44950 Park Rd., Sisseton, SD 57262; (605) 448-5701; https://gfp.sd.gov/parks/

Dog-friendly: Dogs must be on leash or under immediate control
Trail surface/conditions: Forested trail
Land status: Sica Hollow State Park
Nearest town(s): Sisseton
Other trail users: Hikers only
Maps: State park map
Trailhead amenities: Vault toilets, picnic tables
Maximum grade: Negligible

FINDING THE TRAILHEAD

 From the city of Sisseton, head west on SD 10 for a couple of miles until you reach Roberts CR 6. Turn right (north) and proceed 7 miles to CR 12. Turn left (west) and travel 6 miles to the state park (follow signs). The trailhead is located in the park's day-use area. GPS: N45 44.788' / W97 13.099'

THE HIKE

In summer the trail in this woody draw is surrounded by bright green, lush foliage. And with all the deciduous trees at Sica Hollow, hiking in autumn is truly beautiful. Watch for birds such as veeries, chestnut-sided warblers, yellow-bellied sapsuckers, and purple finches.

The hike begins at the trailhead near the day-use area parking lot just past the entrance station. Look for the large wooden sign with "Trail of the Spirits" carved into it. Heading out on the trail, you will immediately cross a footbridge over Roy Creek and start to gently walk uphill. Interpretive signs along the trail provide information about the natural history of the hollow. Once arriving at the steps headed uphill, there are a variety of options as to which direction you can go to complete your hike. Refer to the map and the Miles and Directions for guidance.

MILES AND DIRECTIONS

0.0 Begin at the trailhead sign in the park's day-use area.

0.25 You will reach steps that climb a hill, go right (south) up the steps. **Option:** If you want to avoid the steps, proceeding straight (east) is also an option.

0.35 After making a loop and returning back down on another set of steps, you have three options: turn left (west) and return to the trailhead the way you came; hike on a short cut-across trail that leads directly north to the middle of the day-use area; or, for the hike described here, turn right (east) to complete the entire loop.

0.6 The trail ends on the easternmost side of the day-use area; walk back to your vehicle on the road.

0.8 Arrive back at the trailhead parking lot.

Dense green foliage during summer along the Trail of the Spirits

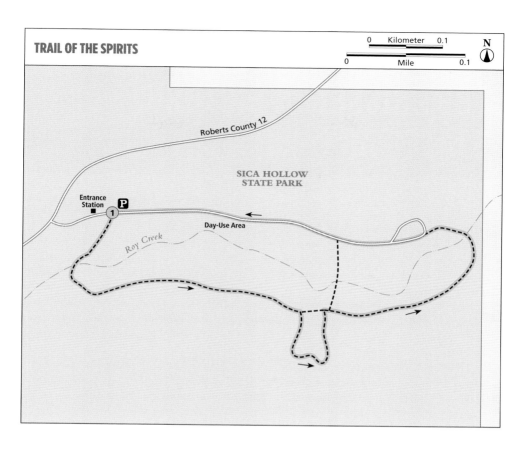

TRAIL OF THE SPIRITS

0   Kilometer   0.1

0   Mile   0.1

N

Roberts County 12

SICA HOLLOW
STATE PARK

Entrance
Station

P

1

Day-Use Area

Roy Creek

FORT SISSETON HISTORIC STATE PARK

Fort Sisseton was established in 1864 and originally given the name Fort Wadsworth; however, its name was changed in 1876 to avoid confusion with Fort Wadsworth, New York. The fort is located on top of the Coteau des Prairies, and the site was chosen because of its natural defensive position, proximity to ample drinking water, and thick forests of trees that could be used for fuel and timber. The US military was stationed at the fort between 1864 and 1889.

Fort Sisseton is listed on the National Register of Historic Places and became a part of South Dakota's state park system in 1959. Visitors to the fort today can see and tour many restored buildings that are still standing, such as the officers' quarters, guardhouse, and barracks.

If visiting around the first full weekend of June, plan to attend the Fort Sisseton Historical Festival for a fun weekend of reenactments, music, and food. According to South Dakota Game, Fish and Parks, more than 15,000 visitors attend the annual event.

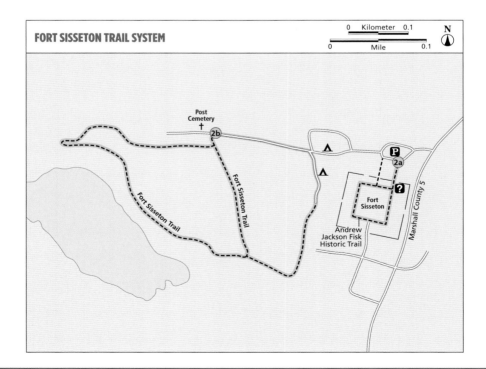

2 FORT SISSETON TRAIL SYSTEM

A short walk around historic Fort Sisseton and an adjacent wetlands area in northeastern South Dakota.

Start: The Andrew Jackson Fisk Trail begins at the park's visitor center, while there are many access points to start hiking on the Fort Sisseton Trail
Elevation gain: 1,773 to 1,843 feet
Distance: 2.0 miles of trails
Difficulty: Easy
Hiking time: 1 to 2 hours
Seasons: Best spring through fall
Fees and permits: Park entrance fee
Trail contact: Fort Sisseton Historic State Park, 11907 434th Ave., Lake City, SD 57247; (605) 448-5474; https://gfp.sd.gov/parks/

Dog-friendly: Dogs must be on leash or under immediate control
Trail surface/conditions: Boardwalk, mowed grass
Land status: Fort Sisseton Historic State Park
Nearest town(s): Lake City, Eden
Other trail users: Mountain bikes allowed on Fort Sisseton Trail
Maps: State park map
Trailhead amenities: Available throughout park
Maximum grade: Negligible

FINDING THE TRAILHEAD

From the town of Eden, head west on Marshall CR 16 for about 5 miles before turning right (north) onto CR 5 for 3 miles to Fort Sisseton. GPS: Andrew Jackson Fisk Trail: N45 39.505' / W97 31.776'; Fort Sisseton Trail: N45 39.586' / W97 32.230'

THE HIKE

For those interested in the history of the American West, a visit to Fort Sisseton is worth the trip. The park has two easy trails.

The Andrew Jackson Fisk Trail is a 0.3-mile historical interpretive trail that leads hikers around the fort to buildings such as the officers' quarters, guardhouse, and barracks. Fisk spent the winter of 1865 at Fort Sisseton as a soldier in Company A of the Second Minnesota Cavalry. During his time at the fort he kept a journal, and passages from his journal are included on interpretive panels along the trail and provide a firsthand account about life at the fort. Make sure to stop in to the park's visitor center (northeast corner of the fort) to visit the museum and pick up a free copy of the *Fort Sisseton Historic State Park Walking Tour Guide*.

Immediately to the west of the fort, the Fort Sisseton Trail loops are 1.7 miles total and explore a prairie wetland area. The westernmost trail loop is 1.1 miles long. A good starting and ending point for the western loop is near the Post Cemetery, which you can drive your vehicle to. Information about the region's natural history is explained on interpretive panels along the trail. Birders would be especially interested to hike the trail, as great blue herons, double-crested cormorants, Canada geese, and pelicans inhabit these prairie pothole wetlands of South Dakota.

Cannon at Fort Sisseton JOHN MITCHELL

The officers' quarters at Fort Sisseton

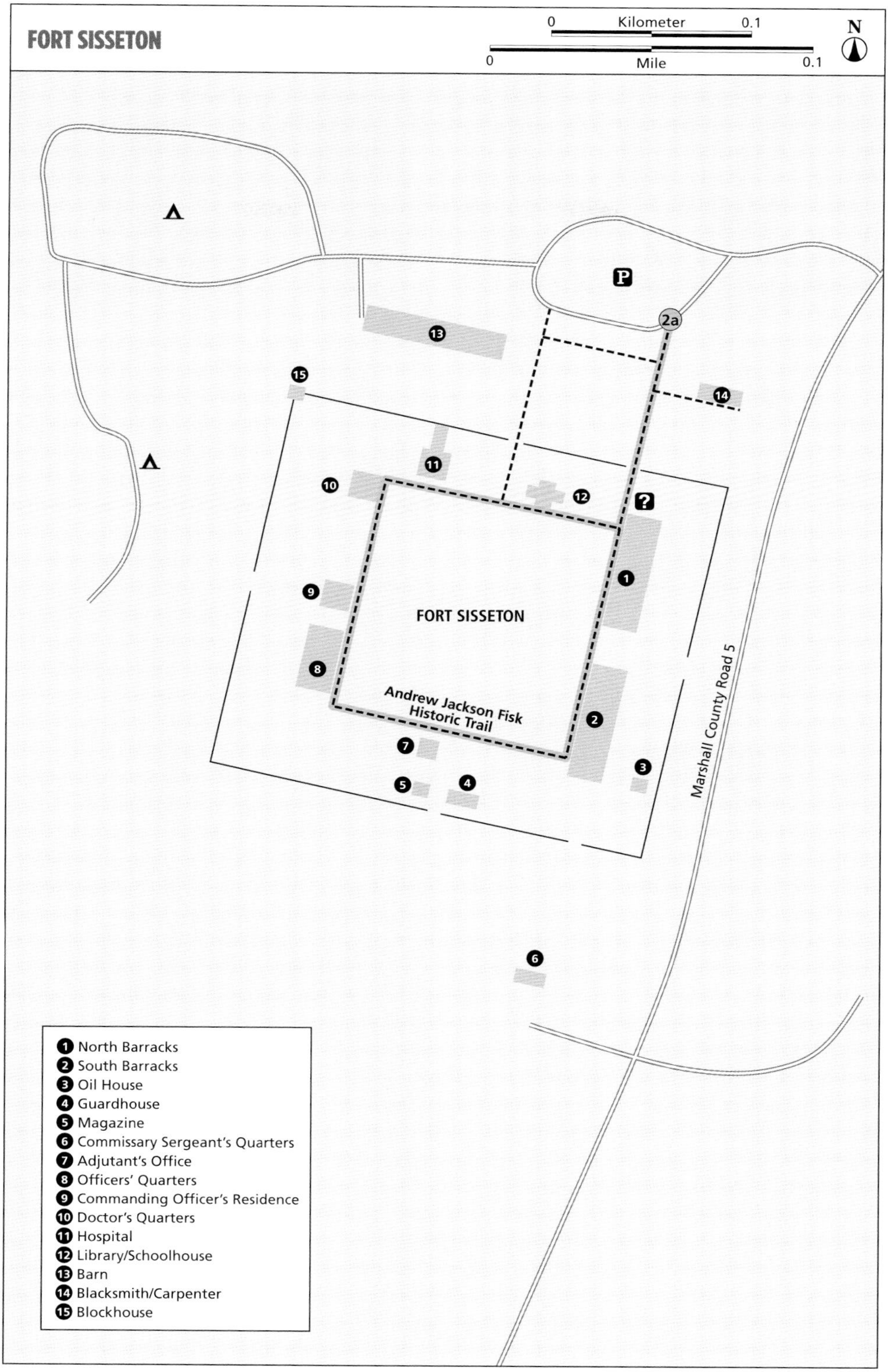

FORT SISSETON

0   Kilometer   0.1

0   Mile   0.1

N

P

2a

14

13

15

11

10

12

?

1

FORT SISSETON

9

Andrew Jackson Fisk
Historic Trail

8

2

7

3

Marshall County Road 5

5   **4**

6

1 North Barracks
2 South Barracks
3 Oil House
4 Guardhouse
5 Magazine
6 Commissary Sergeant's Quarters
7 Adjutant's Office
8 Officers' Quarters
9 Commanding Officer's Residence
10 Doctor's Quarters
11 Hospital
12 Library/Schoolhouse
13 Barn
14 Blacksmith/Carpenter
15 Blockhouse

WAUBAY NATIONAL WILDLIFE REFUGE

According to the US Fish & Wildlife Service, Waubay translates to "where wildfowl build their nests" in the Lakota Sioux language. This is definitely true, as the 4,650-acre refuge is home to more than 100 species of songbirds, game birds, and waterfowl. Additionally, at least 140 other species of birds temporarily make the refuge their home during annual migrations. While birding, look for birds such as western grebes, American white pelicans, snowy egrets, and the possible rare sighting of a white-winged scoter.

The refuge, which was established in 1935 by President Franklin D. Roosevelt, encompasses grasslands, woodlands, marshes, and lakes that are also home to white-tailed deer, coyotes, red foxes, and woodchucks (groundhogs). Begin your tour of the refuge with a stop at the Headquarters Island Visitor Center to learn more about the area's history and wildlife. The refuge grounds are only open during daylight hours. Hikers are requested to stay on designated trails.

HEADQUARTERS ISLAND TRAIL SYSTEM

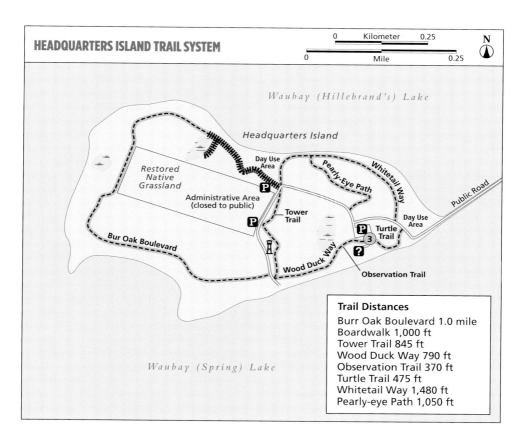

Trail Distances

Burr Oak Boulevard 1.0 mile
Boardwalk 1,000 ft
Tower Trail 845 ft
Wood Duck Way 790 ft
Observation Trail 370 ft
Turtle Trail 475 ft
Whitetail Way 1,480 ft
Pearly-eye Path 1,050 ft

3 HEADQUARTERS ISLAND TRAIL SYSTEM

A series of short interpretive trails that lead hikers around Headquarters Island at Waubay National Wildlife Refuge.

Start: At one of three public parking lots on Headquarters Island (see map)
Elevation gain: Little to none
Distance: Approximately 2.0 miles of trails (vary from 370 feet to 1.0 mile)
Difficulty: Easy
Hiking time: Anywhere from 5 minutes to 2 hours
Seasons: Best spring through fall
Fees and permits: No fees or permits required
Trail contact: Waubay National Wildlife Refuge, 44401 134A St., Waubay, SD 57273; (605) 947-4521; https://www.fws.gov/refuge/Waubay/

Dog-friendly: Leashed dogs permitted
Trail surface/conditions: Forested trail, boardwalk
Land status: Waubay National Wildlife Refuge
Nearest town(s): Waubay
Other trail users: Hikers only; bikes limited to public roads
Maps: Printed maps available at visitor center and on signage throughout refuge; trail maps also posted online
Trailhead amenities: Available throughout refuge
Maximum grade: Negligible

FINDING THE TRAILHEAD

From the town of Waubay, head east on US 12 to Day CR 1. Turn left (north) and drive for about 7 miles, then follow signs to Headquarters Island. *Note:* Entering the refuge's official trail contact address into your GPS system will not lead you to Headquarters Island. Follow these directions. GPS: refuge headquarters and visitor center N45 25.499' / W97 19.585'

THE HIKE

Headquarters Island is a fun place to explore by foot on the island's well-marked trail system. All of the trails are named (with appropriate names such as Whitetail Way and Bur Oak Boulevard) and given a specific color on refuge maps and signage, making wayfinding easy for hikers. A trip up to the top of the observation tower is well worth it, if you are not afraid of heights. From the top of the 110-foot tower, you can see the prairie pothole lakes dotting the landscape. Wearing insect repellent is strongly recommended while hiking on Headquarters Island.

December at Waubay National Wildlife Refuge TRAVEL SOUTH DAKOTA

HARTFORD BEACH STATE PARK

Hartford Beach State Park is a popular destination in northeastern South Dakota for hikers, bikers, cross-country skiers, swimmers, campers, and boaters. The park is located on the South Dakota–Minnesota border on the southern shore of Big Stone Lake. Scenic bluffs and forested shorelines provide excellent hiking opportunities at the 331–acre park.

Native American cultural sites as well as more recent French and English fur trapping histories exist throughout the area, and the park explains these both on its well-marked interpretive trails. Native American burial mounds that date from between 300 CE and 1600 CE can be observed in the park. Please be respectful of these important cultural sites.

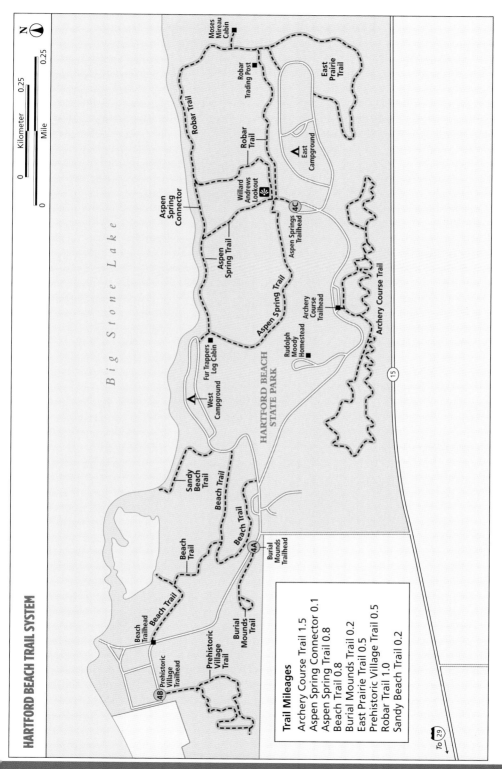

Trail Mileages

Archery Course Trail 1.5
Aspen Spring Connector 0.1
Aspen Spring Trail 0.8
Beach Trail 0.8
Burial Mounds Trail 0.2
East Prairie Trail 0.5
Prehistoric Village Trail 0.5
Robar Trail 1.0
Sandy Beach Trail 0.2

4 HARTFORD BEACH TRAIL SYSTEM

An extensive trail system that leads hikers to the top of bluffs, through woods, and along shorelines. Historic sites are located throughout the park.

Start: At one of many trailheads located throughout the park (see map)
Elevation gain: 966 to 1,103 feet
Distance: Approximately 5.6 miles of trails
Difficulty: Easy to moderate
Hiking time: Anywhere from 15 minutes to a half day
Seasons: Best spring through fall
Fees and permits: Park entrance fee
Trail contact: Hartford Beach State Park, 13672 Hartford Beach Rd., Corona, SD 57227; (605) 432-6374; https://gfp.sd.gov/parks/

Dog-friendly: Dogs must be on leash or under immediate control
Trail surface/conditions: Forested trail, mowed grass
Land status: Hartford Beach State Park
Nearest town(s): Big Stone City, Milbank, Wilmot
Other trail users: Mountain bikers
Maps: State park map
Trailhead amenities: Available throughout park
Maximum grade: Varies

FINDING THE TRAILHEAD

From the junction of US 12 and SD 15 in the city of Milbank, head north on SD 15 for 14 miles to the state park. GPS: N45 23.903' / W96 40.374'

THE HIKE

Of all the trails at Hartford Beach, the Burial Mounds Trail, Prehistoric Village Trail, and the Aspen Spring Trail stand out the most.

The Burial Mounds Trail is located almost immediately to the west of the park's entrance station. The short, 0.2-mile lollipop trail leads to a Native American burial mound. The mound at the end of the trail was excavated by archaeologist Dr. William Henry Over in 1922. In his field notes, he wrote:

> The mound we excavated [. . .] is one of a string of mounds on the brow of this high terrace overlooking the west shore of Big Stone Lake. The mound is 54 feet in diameter, 6 feet high and the largest one so far investigated. In all, 14 skeletons [. . .] had been buried here and later the mound erected. Those found here in a sitting posture were complete and had been deposited at the time of death.

The 0.5-mile Prehistoric Village Trail on the park's western boundary leads hikers to the top of a ridge that overlooks Big Stone Lake and to a prehistoric village. Archaeologists who excavated the site in the 1980s discovered several bone tools, clamshells, stone artifacts, a clay pipe, and numerous other items of interest.

The 0.8-mile Aspen Spring Trail loop is a scenic hike through the woods of Hartford Beach, beginning on top of a ridge and then descending to the shoreline. In summer, the foliage is lush and you will hear the sound of running water from the area's springs. Also be on the lookout for birds such as pileated woodpeckers, scarlet tanagers, and great crested flycatchers. The water in this area once attracted animals such as bison, bears, and wolves.

Boardwalk along the Aspen Spring Trail

Flowing water along the Aspen Spring Trail

OAKWOOD LAKES STATE PARK

Eight glacial lakes make up this unique state park in eastern South Dakota. According to South Dakota Game, Fish and Parks, the lakes at Oakwood "were formed more than 10,000 years ago when melting glaciers filled depressions scooped in the earth's surface by advancing ice." The chain of lakes with its surrounding forests and fertile lands attracted both Native American and Euro-American settlers to the area. There are possibly up to ten Native American burial mounds from the Woodland culture in the area, three of which can be found just off the park's main road past the entrance station. Please be respectful of these important cultural sites.

Oakwood Lakes is probably the one state park I have spent the most time at in my entire life. It seems like a long time ago now, but after high school, I attended South Dakota State University in Brookings, about a 25-minute drive away from Oakwood Lakes. I spent much of my free time in college exploring the park by foot or on my bike, swimming, fishing, and watching the sunset over Lake Tetonkaha (sometimes I studied, too). Sitting on the lake's eastern shore and watching the entire western horizon turn a deep purple in the evening is something I will not forget. If spending a night camping in the park, allow yourself to take some time to disconnect and watch the sun dip below the calm lake waters of Oakwood.

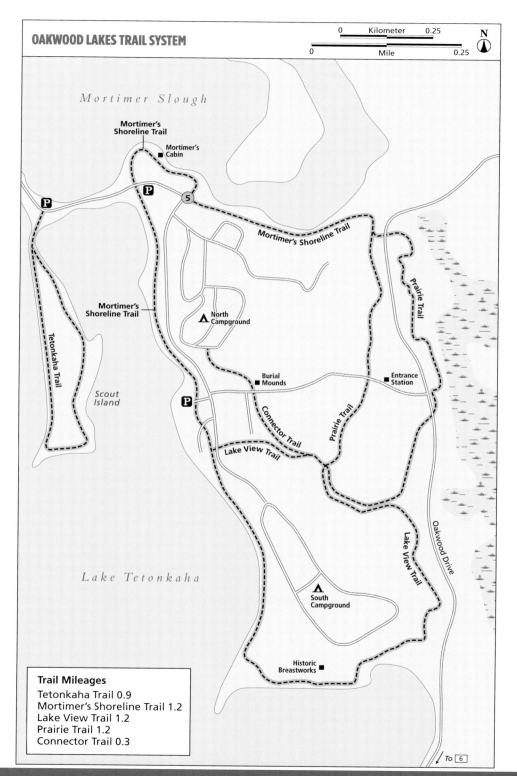

OAKWOOD LAKES TRAIL SYSTEM

Mortimer Slough

Mortimer's Shoreline Trail

Mortimer's Cabin

5

Mortimer's Shoreline Trail

Mortimer's Shoreline Trail

Prairie Trail

Tetonkaha Trail

North Campground

Scout Island

Burial Mounds

Entrance Station

Connector Trail

Prairie Trail

Lake View Trail

Lake Tetonkaha

South Campground

Lake View Trail

Oakwood Drive

Historic Breastworks

Trail Mileages
Tetonkaha Trail 0.9
Mortimer's Shoreline Trail 1.2
Lake View Trail 1.2
Prairie Trail 1.2
Connector Trail 0.3

0   Kilometer   0.25
0   Mile   0.25

N

To 6

5 OAKWOOD LAKES TRAIL SYSTEM

A series of trails leading hikers through a varied landscape between eight interconnected lakes in eastern South Dakota.

Start: At one of the many parking areas located near the trails (see map)
Elevation gain: 1,616 to 1,670 feet
Distance: 4.8 miles of trails
Difficulty: Easy to moderate
Hiking time: 30 minutes to 2 hours
Seasons: Best spring through fall
Fees and permits: Park entrance fee
Trail contact: Oakwood Lakes State Park, 20247 Oakwood Dr., Bruce, SD 57220; (605) 627-5441; https://gfp.sd.gov/parks/
Dog-friendly: Dogs must be on leash or under immediate control

Trail surface/conditions: Forested trail, dirt path, mowed grass
Land status: Oakwood Lakes State Park
Nearest town(s): Arlington, Volga, Brookings, Bruce
Other trail users: Mountain bikers, horseback riders, cross-country skiers, snowshoers
Maps: State park map
Trailhead amenities: Available throughout park
Maximum grade: Negligible

FINDING THE TRAILHEAD

From the city of Arlington, take US 81 north to Brookings CR 6. Turn right (east) on CR 6 and travel approximately 7 miles to Oakwood Drive. Head north on this road and follow signs to the state park. GPS: N44 26.969' / W96 58.857'

THE HIKE

The eight interconnected lakes that make up Oakwood Lakes are Lake Tetonkaha, Upper Lake Tetonkaha, Round Lake, Turtle Lake, Johnson Lake, Mortimer Slough, Walters Lake, and East Lake Oakwood. Many of the park's trails are alongside the lakes, but some venture across open prairie areas. The trails also lead to historic sites such as Native American burial mounds, breastworks built by the US military in 1859, and Samuel "Ol Spot" Mortimer's log cabin.

Tetonkaha translates to "place of the great summer lodge" in the Sioux language. The Sioux visited this area seasonally to hunt and fish. Later Euro-American settlers named the area "Oakwood" because of the clusters of oak trees here.

While hiking, be on the lookout for birds such as green herons, yellow- and black-billed cuckoos, and northern cardinals.

View of Lake Tetonkaha at Oakwood Lakes

Samuel "Ol Spot" Mortimer's cabin

LAKE HERMAN STATE PARK

According to South Dakota Game, Fish and Parks, glacial ice melt occurring thousands of years ago formed the 1,350-acre Lake Herman. Located west of the city of Madison, the state park sits on a peninsula that juts out from the eastern shore of Lake Herman, offering visitors wonderful views of the water and surrounding area. The park is a popular destination for hiking, biking, fishing, boating, canoeing, kayaking, swimming, and disc golf. It is named for Herman Luce, reported to be one of the first Euro-American settlers of the area. The park has three marked trails: the Abott Trail, Luce Adventure Trail, and the Pioneer Adventure Trail.

LAKE HERMAN TRAIL SYSTEM

0   Kilometer 0.25

0   Mile   0.25

N

Pioneer Adventure Trailhead

Entrance
Station

Day Use
Area

Luce
Cabin

Pioneer
Adventure
Trail

Lake Herman

Luce Adventure
Trailhead

*Herman
Pond*

Luce
Adventure
Trail

Pioneer Adventure Trail

Beach

Fishing
Dock

Abott
Trailhead

6

Beach

Day Use
Area

Abott Trail

Trail Mileages

Abott Trail 1.0
Luce Adventure Trail 1.3
Pioneer Adventure Trail 0.9

6 LAKE HERMAN TRAIL SYSTEM

A series of trails that lead hikers through prairie grasses, around Herman Pond, and up hills that offer great views of Lake Herman.

Start: At one of the many parking areas located near the trails (see map)
Elevation gain: 1,669 to 1,753 feet
Distance: 3.2 miles of trails
Difficulty: Easy to moderate
Hiking time: 30 minutes to 2 hours
Seasons: Best spring through fall
Fees and permits: Park entrance fee
Trail contact: Lake Herman State Park, 23409 State Park Dr., Madison, SD 57042; (605) 256-5003; https://gfp.sd.gov/parks/

Dog-friendly: Dogs must be on leash or under immediate control
Trail surface/conditions: Forested trail, dirt path, mowed grass
Land status: Lake Herman State Park
Nearest town(s): Madison
Other trail users: Mountain bikers, cross-country skiers, snowshoers
Maps: State park map
Trailhead amenities: Available throughout park
Maximum grade: Negligible

FINDING THE TRAILHEAD

From the city of Madison, take SD 34 west for a couple of miles to Lake CR 38, turn left (south), and follow signs to state park. GPS: Abott Trail, N43 59.090' / W97 09.569'; Luce Adventure Trail, N43 59.323' / W97 10.073'; Pioneer Adventure Trail, N43 59.563' / W97 09.573'

THE HIKE

Lake Herman State Park has three interpretive trails that explore different aspects of the park.

The Pioneer Adventure Trail mostly explores the prairie grasslands on the eastern side of the park. The Luce Adventure Trail is a 1.3-mile hike around Herman Pond with a stop at Herman Luce's historic cabin. The Abott Trail is a 1.0-mile loop through forests and up to a ridgeline that provides excellent views of Lake Herman. This is a great place to watch the sunset.

Birders should be on the lookout for warblers, meadowlarks, herons, blue jays, owls, hawks, horned larks, and pelicans while hiking the trails at Lake Herman.

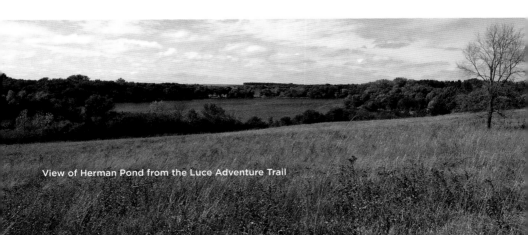

View of Herman Pond from the Luce Adventure Trail

SOUTHEAST

The historic 1908 Palisades Bridge spanning Split Rock Creek at Palisades State Park

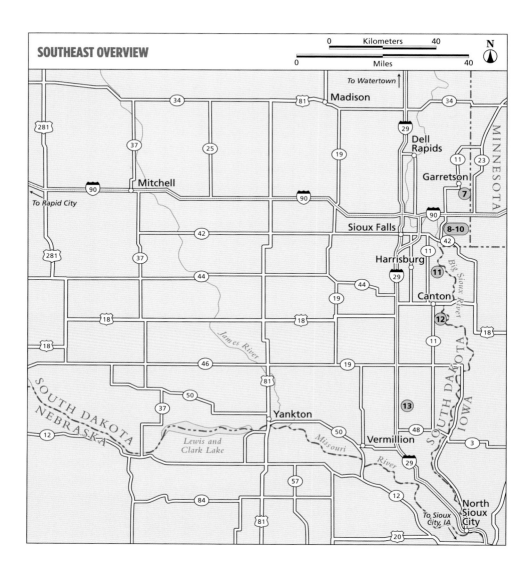

SOUTHEAST OVERVIEW

To Watertown

Madison

To Rapid City

Mitchell

Dell Rapids

Garretson

Sioux Falls

Harrisburg

Canton

Yankton

Lewis and Clark Lake

Vermillion

North Sioux City

To Sioux City, IA

MINNESOTA

SOUTH DAKOTA

NEBRASKA

SOUTH DAKOTA

IOWA

James River

Big Sioux River

Missouri River

PALISADES STATE PARK

Perhaps one of the most scenic settings in all of South Dakota, Palisades State Park is a popular destination for hikers, rock climbers, campers, photographers, and picnickers. Unique Sioux quartzite formations line the banks of Split Rock Creek, which flows through the park. While hiking, make sure to watch your footing. Several high cliffs, bluffs, and rock formations provide picturesque overlooks.

According to South Dakota Game, Fish and Parks (SD GFP), Split Rock Creek cut gorges through this area for millions of years, providing the interesting rock formations that still stand today. The Sioux quartzite spires are estimated to be 1.2 billion years old.

Devils Gulch

The popularity of the park has led the state to propose improvements and possible expansion at Palisades. Additional camping spots and hiking trails may be added in the future. Check the SD GFP website for the most up-to-date information (https://gfp .sd.gov/parks/).

When in the area, also plan a visit to Devils Gulch Park in nearby Garretson. Short walking trails lead you to areas filled with scenic beauty and historical legends. In 1876, American West outlaw Jesse James reportedly jumped his horse over an 18-foot gap at Devils Gulch to elude capture by the authorities.

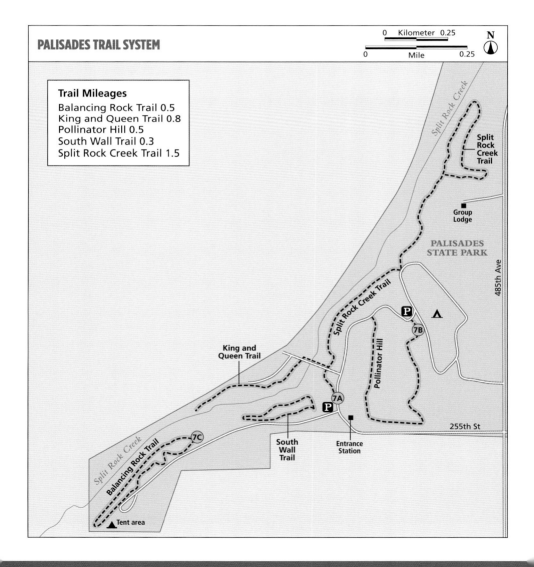

PALISADES TRAIL SYSTEM

0   Kilometer 0.25
0   Mile   0.25
N

Trail Mileages
Balancing Rock Trail 0.5
King and Queen Trail 0.8
Pollinator Hill 0.5
South Wall Trail 0.3
Split Rock Creek Trail 1.5

Split Rock Creek

Split Rock Creek Trail

Group Lodge

PALISADES STATE PARK

485th Ave

Split Rock Creek Trail

King and Queen Trail

Pollinator Hill

7B

7A

South Wall Trail

Entrance Station

255th St

Split Rock Creek

Balancing Rock Trail

7C

Tent area

7 PALISADES TRAIL SYSTEM

A series of short trails that lead hikers to impressive views of the Sioux quartzite formations along Split Rock Creek in southeastern South Dakota.

Start: At one of the three trailheads located in the park (see map)
Elevation gain: 1,394 to 1,513 feet
Distance: 3.6 miles of trails
Difficulty: Easy to moderate
Hiking time: Anywhere from 20 minutes to a half day of exploring
Seasons: Best late spring through fall
Fees and permits: Park entrance fee
Trail contact: Palisades State Park, 25491 485th Ave., Garretson, SD 57030; (605) 594-3824; https://gfp.sd.gov/parks/

Dog-friendly: Dogs must be on leash or under immediate control
Trail surface/conditions: Forested trail, wood chips, mowed grass, rocks
Land status: Palisades State Park
Nearest town(s): Garretson
Other trail users: Hikers only
Maps: State park map
Trailhead amenities: Available throughout park
Maximum grade: Negligible

FINDING THE TRAILHEAD

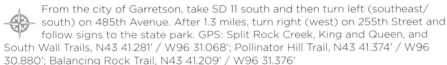

From the city of Garretson, take SD 11 south and then turn left (southeast/south) on 485th Avenue. After 1.3 miles, turn right (west) on 255th Street and follow signs to the state park. GPS: Split Rock Creek, King and Queen, and South Wall Trails, N43 41.281' / W96 31.068'; Pollinator Hill Trail, N43 41.374' / W96 30.880'; Balancing Rock Trail, N43 41.209' / W96 31.376'

THE HIKE

Palisades State Park has five hiking trails: Split Rock Creek Trail, Pollinator Hill Trail, King and Queen Trail, South Wall Trail, and Balancing Rock Trail. The Split Rock Creek, King and Queen, and South Wall Trails can all be accessed from the parking lot just past the park's entrance station.

The 1.5-mile Split Rock Creek Trail leads hikers in a north/northeasterly direction along the banks of Split Rock Creek, offering scenic views of the creek, the historic 1908 bridge, and Sioux quartzite formations. Watch your footing while hiking along the creek, as there are numerous slippery rocks that you will have to walk over.

The King and Queen Trail is a 0.8-mile out-and-back trail that leads hikers across the 1908 bridge and then in a southwesterly direction along the north side of the creek to up-close views of the King and Queen Rocks.

The South Wall Trail is a 0.3-mile loop that leads hikers to a scenic area overlooking the King and Queen Rocks.

The Pollinator Hill Trail shows a different side of the park, leading hikers through prairie grasses on the 0.5-mile loop. The trail begins behind the campground's comfort station near the amphitheater.

The 0.5-mile Balancing Rock Trail is accessed just a short way down the park's gravel road to the southwest and, as its name suggests, leads to a rock formation that appears to be balancing.

Palisades State Park is an especially scenic place to be during sunrise and sunset.

Sunrise on Split Rock Creek

View of the King and Queen Rocks as seen from the South Wall Trail

BIG SIOUX RECREATION AREA

Established in 1978, this 430-acre park is a popular destination for hikers, canoers, bicyclists, campers, and archers. The recreation area is located near the cities of Sioux Falls and Brandon in southeastern South Dakota. The large hill on the park's western side is a part of the southern portion of the Coteau des Prairies. A hike to the top of the ridge via the Prairie Vista Trail rewards hikers with excellent views of the surrounding area. The Big Sioux River, which flows through the middle of the park, is a popular place to canoe, kayak, and fish. Cross-country skiing, snowshoeing, and snowmobiling in the park are common activities in the winter.

While spending time in the park, look for birds such as solitary sandpipers, red-bellied woodpeckers, eastern screech-owls, and yellow-throated vireos.

Note: This area is prone to flooding in spring.

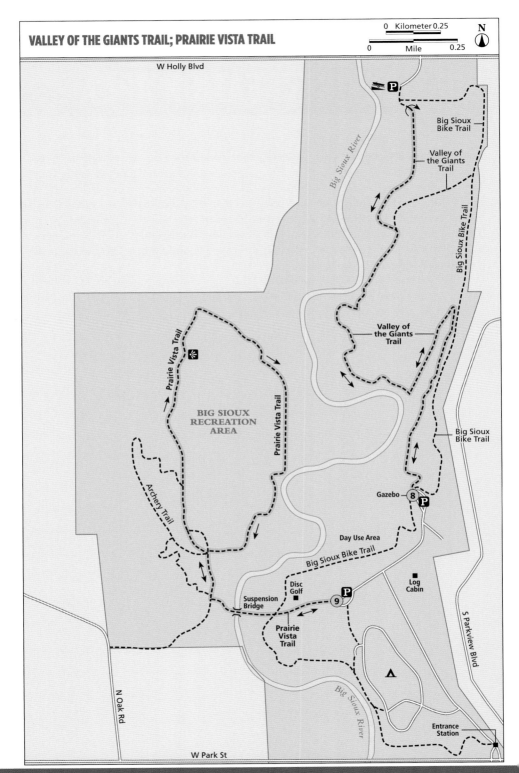

VALLEY OF THE GIANTS TRAIL; PRAIRIE VISTA TRAIL

W Holly Blvd

N

0 Kilometer 0.25

0 Mile 0.25

Big Sioux River

Big Sioux Bike Trail

Valley of the Giants Trail

Big Sioux Bike Trail

Prairie Vista Trail

Valley of the Giants Trail

BIG SIOUX RECREATION AREA

Prairie Vista Trail

Archery Trail

Big Sioux Bike Trail

Gazebo 8 P

Day Use Area

Big Sioux Bike Trail

Log Cabin

Suspension Bridge

Disc Golf

P 9

Prairie Vista Trail

S Parkview Blvd

N Oak Rd

Big Sioux River

Entrance Station

W Park St

8 VALLEY OF THE GIANTS TRAIL

A walk among giant trees located in a floodplain along the Big Sioux River near Sioux Falls.

Start: At the Valley of the Giants trailhead near the park's gazebo
Elevation gain: 1,295 to 1,342 feet
Distance: 3.2 miles out and back
Difficulty: Easy to moderate
Hiking time: 1 to 2 hours
Seasons: All
Fees and permits: Park entrance fee
Trail contact: Big Sioux Recreation Area, 410 W. Park St., Brandon, SD 57005; (605) 582-7243; https://gfp.sd.gov/parks/

Dog-friendly: Dogs must be on leash or under immediate control
Trail surface/conditions: Forested trail, mowed grass
Land status: Big Sioux State Recreation Area
Nearest town(s): Brandon, Sioux Falls
Other trail users: Cross-country skiers, snowshoers
Maps: State park map
Trailhead amenities: Available throughout park
Maximum grade: Negligible

FINDING THE TRAILHEAD

From the city of Brandon, head south on SD 11 and turn right (north) on South Sioux Boulevard. After only 0.3 mile, turn left (west) on West Park Street and follow signs to the state park. Once in the park, follow signage to the Valley of the Giants trailhead. GPS: N43 34.858' / W96 35.863'

THE HIKE

This is a wonderful hike through the tall trees along the Big Sioux River. The hike begins near the park's gazebo. At first you will parallel the paved Big Sioux Bike Trail, but after making a big U-turn, you will descend to the river. At about 0.7 mile, the trail begins to head in a northwesterly direction among the trees. Just after a mile of hiking, the trail leaves the shade and heads north through tall grasses. This section can be hot during the summer months. At 1.5 miles, you will reach the north canoe launch. From here, you have a couple options: You can hike back the way you came or take the bike path back to the gazebo.

Note: Bikes are not allowed on the Valley of the Giants Trail.

MILES AND DIRECTIONS

0.0 Start at the trailhead near the park's gazebo.

0.45 The trail makes a big U-turn.

0.7 You have reached the banks of the Big Sioux River; turn right and head in a north-westerly direction among tall trees.

1.1 The trail enters a large grassy area and heads north.

1.2 Trail split; keep left (west/north). The trail leading to the northeast connects with the paved bike path.

1.6 You have reached the end of the trail at the north canoe launch; retrace your steps to the trailhead. ***Option:*** You can also take the paved bike path back to the trailhead.

3.2 Arrive back at the trailhead.

The first portion of the Valley of the Giants Trail is heavily forested

9 PRAIRIE VISTA TRAIL

A hike to the top of the Coteau des Prairies, offering wonderful views of the surrounding area. The trail can be quite hot in summer. See map on page 72.

Start: At the trailhead in the park's day-use area
Elevation gain: 1,287 to 1,442 feet
Distance: 2.1-mile lollipop
Difficulty: Moderate
Hiking time: 1 to 2 hours
Seasons: All
Fees and permits: Park entrance fee
Trail contact: Big Sioux Recreation Area, 410 W. Park St., Brandon, SD 57005; (605) 582-7243; https://gfp.sd.gov/parks/
Dog-friendly: Dogs must be on leash or under immediate control

Trail surface/conditions: Mowed grass, forested trail
Land status: Big Sioux State Recreation Area
Nearest town(s): Brandon, Sioux Falls
Other trail users: Mountain bikers, horseback riders, cross-country skiers, snowshoers (snowmobiles allowed on trail in winter)
Maps: State park map
Trailhead amenities: Available throughout park
Maximum grade: 5.4% for 0.5 mile

FINDING THE TRAILHEAD

 From the city of Brandon, head south on SD 11 and turn right (north) on South Sioux Boulevard. After only 0.3 mile, turn left (west) on West Park Street and follow signs to the state park. Once in the park, follow signage to the Prairie Vista trailhead. GPS: N43 34.668' / W96 36.065'

THE HIKE

The Prairie Vista Trail begins at the park's day-use area, and at first the trail is shaded by large trees. Before reaching the loop portion, the trail crosses over a bike path as well as a suspension bridge across the Big Sioux River, and also traverses through the park's disc golf course.

At 0.3 mile, the trail links up with the Archery Trail; make sure to keep right (north) to remain on the Prairie Vista Trail. Only 0.1 mile later, the loop section of the trail is reached, and you have a choice of either proceeding straight up the ridgeline or taking a hard right turn (east) to hike along the river first, then up the ridgeline later. The described route has you getting the hard part over with, hiking up to the top of the hill first.

A rest bench greets you at the top, so take a few moments to look out over the Big Sioux River valley. From here, the trail descends and loops back around to close the loop. You will then hike back to the day-use area the same way you came.

MILES AND DIRECTIONS

0.0 Start at the trailhead in the park's day-use area.

0.2 Cross suspension bridge across the Big Sioux River.

0.3 Junction with Archery Trail; keep right (north).

0.4 The loop begins; proceed in a northerly direction up the hill.

0.55 Second junction with the Archery Trail; remain on Prairie Vista Trail heading north.

0.9 A rest bench is reached at the top of the ridgeline.

1.7 Close the loop and turn left (south) to retrace your steps back to the trailhead.

2.1 Arrive back at the trailhead.

Sunset along the Prairie Vista Trail ANDREW PESCHONG

BEAVER CREEK NATURE AREA

Located just east of the Big Sioux Recreation Area (page 71), the Beaver Creek Nature Area is a wonderful spot to relax and enjoy the outdoors in a scenic setting. Beaver Creek, named by early Euro-American settlers for the large number of beavers living along the creek, begins across the state border in Minnesota and ends when it flows into nearby Split Rock Creek, the same creek that flows through Palisades State Park (page 67). Wildlife that can be found at Beaver Creek includes white-tailed deer, foxes, rabbits, woodchucks (groundhogs), and beavers.

The park has two trails: the Homestead Loop Trail and the Homesteader Nature Trail. The Homestead Loop Trail is a short, 0.2-mile accessible trail that makes a loop around a historic 1872 cabin that was built by homesteaders John and Anna Samuelson. The Homesteader Nature Trail leads hikers through forests, prairies, and creek bottoms as it winds its way through the southern portion of the nature area.

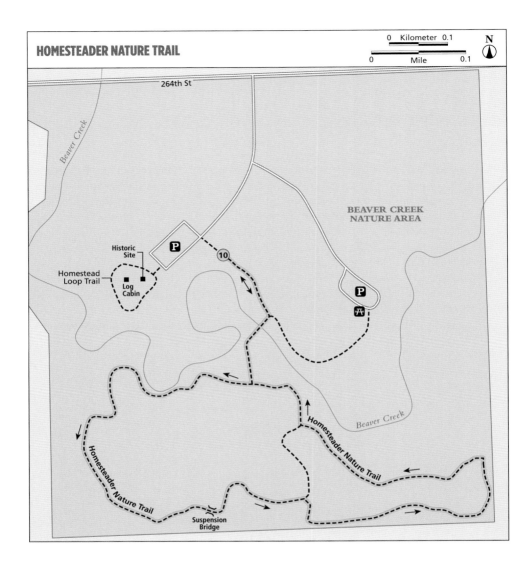

10 HOMESTEADER NATURE TRAIL

A fun interpretive trail through dense woods along Beaver Creek in southeastern South Dakota.

Start: At the trailhead southeast of the nature area parking lot
Elevation gain: 1,326 to 1,404 feet
Distance: 1.4-mile lollipop
Difficulty: Easy
Hiking time: 30 minutes to 1 hour
Seasons: Best spring through fall
Fees and permits: No fees or permits required
Trail contact: Beaver Creek Nature Area, 48351 264th St., Valley Springs, SD 57068; (605) 594-3824; https://gfp.sd.gov/parks/

Dog-friendly: Dogs must be on leash or under immediate control
Trail surface/conditions: Forested trail, mowed grass
Land status: Beaver Creek Nature Area
Nearest town(s): Brandon
Other trail users: Hikers only
Maps: State park map
Trailhead amenities: Vault toilet, picnic tables
Maximum grade: Negligible

FINDING THE TRAILHEAD

From the city of Brandon, head east on East Aspen Boulevard/Minnehaha CR 138. After about 2 miles, turn right (south) onto 484th Avenue/Minnehaha CR 109. After 2 more miles, turn right (west) on 264th Street and follow signs to the nature area. GPS: N43 33.340' / W96 32.556'

THE HIKE

This hike is suitable for the entire family. The trail leads hikers along densely wooded Beaver Creek and through prairie grasses in the southeastern section of the park.

The hike begins to the southeast of the parking lot in a grassy area (look for signage). After only 0.1 mile of walking, you will reach a junction; keep right (south/southwest) and cross the bridge over Beaver Creek.

At the next junction, also keep to the right (west). This is the beginning of the loop. The trail will take you through the gently rolling, forested hills, over a suspension bridge, and through prairie grasses before returning to this spot. Watch for signs of wildlife while hiking.

Social trails abound here; make sure to stay on designated trails (which will usually be the wider paths).

MILES AND DIRECTIONS

0.0 Start at the trailhead across from the parking lot in a grassy area (look for signage).

0.1 Trail junction; keep right (south/southwest) and cross bridge over Beaver Creek.

0.15 This trail junction is the beginning of the loop; keep right (west). There is a rest bench at this site.

0.6 Cross a suspension bridge.

0.7 Trail junction; keep right (in an easterly direction) to continue on the loop. This section of trail leads through the prairie. **Option:** Turning left (north) will lead back to the trailhead.

1.2 Trail junction; keep right (north).

1.25 Arrive back at the beginning of the loop where the rest bench is located. Turn right (north)

1.3 Cross the bridge over Beaver Creek and arrive at a junction; turn left (northwest).

1.4 Arrive back at the trailhead.

Suspension bridge along the Beaver Creek Homesteader Nature Trail

GOOD EARTH STATE PARK

Good Earth State Park is a part of the National Historical Landmark Blood Run. This was one of the oldest sites of long-term human habitation in the United States between 1300–1700 CE. The area had a good source of water (the Big Sioux River), fertile lands, protection from harsh weather, and abundant wildlife. Additionally, it was an important ceremonial site and trading center for numerous Native American nations. The main occupants were the Omaha, Ponca, Ioway and Otoe tribes. In 2013, Good Earth State Park became South Dakota's thirteenth state park. When visiting, please be respectful of this important site.

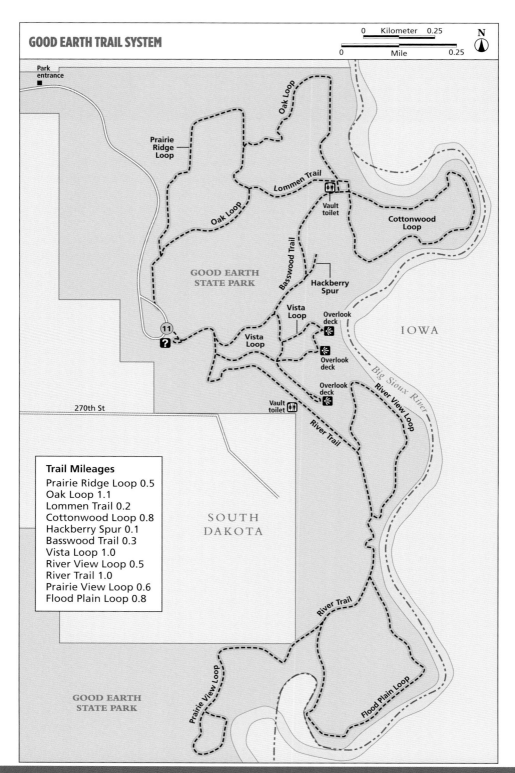

GOOD EARTH TRAIL SYSTEM

0 Kilometer 0.25

0 Mile 0.25

N

Park entrance

Oak Loop

Prairie Ridge Loop

Lommen Trail

Vault toilet

Oak Loop

Cottonwood Loop

Basswood Trail

GOOD EARTH STATE PARK

Hackberry Spur

Vista Loop

Overlook deck

IOWA

Vista Loop

Overlook deck

Big Sioux River

Overlook deck

River View Loop

270th St

Vault toilet

River Trail

Trail Mileages
Prairie Ridge Loop 0.5
Oak Loop 1.1
Lommen Trail 0.2
Cottonwood Loop 0.8
Hackberry Spur 0.1
Basswood Trail 0.3
Vista Loop 1.0
River View Loop 0.5
River Trail 1.0
Prairie View Loop 0.6
Flood Plain Loop 0.8

SOUTH DAKOTA

River Trail

Prairie View Loop

GOOD EARTH STATE PARK

Flood Plain Loop

11 GOOD EARTH TRAIL SYSTEM

A series of trails leading hikers through forests and prairies along the banks of the Big Sioux River on the border of South Dakota and Iowa. Before hiking, be sure to stop in to the visitor center museum to learn more about this historical place.

Start: At the visitor center parking lot
Elevation gain: 1,227 to 1,448 feet
Distance: 6.9 miles of trails
Difficulty: Easy to moderate
Hiking time: 30 minutes to a full day
Seasons: Best spring through fall
Fees and permits: Park entrance fee
Trail contact: Good Earth State Park, 26924 480th Ave., Sioux Falls, SD 57108; (605) 213-1036; https://gfp .sd.gov/parks/

Dog-friendly: Dogs must be on leash or under immediate control
Trail surface/conditions: Forested trail, mowed grass
Land status: Good Earth State Park
Nearest town(s): Sioux Falls, Harrisburg
Other trail users: Hikers only
Maps: State park map
Trailhead amenities: Available at visitor center
Maximum grade: Varies

FINDING THE TRAILHEAD

From the city of Sioux Falls, take SD 42 east until it intersects SD 11. Turn right (south) onto SD 11 and drive approximately 4 miles, then turn left (east) onto Lincoln CR 102. Follow this road for 2 miles, then turn right (south) onto CR 135. After only 0.2 mile, look for the state park entrance on your left (to the east). Follow the road to the visitor center parking lot. GPS: N43 28.643' / W96 35.673'

THE HIKE

The trails at Good Earth State Park are well marked and offer much variety as they lead hikers to scenic overlooks, through forests and prairies, and along the banks of the Big Sioux River. Interpretive panels along the trails explain the area's geology, history, and ecology.

Take a look at the trail map of Good Earth to determine which loops you want to make while exploring the park. If you only have a short time to spend at the park, consider hiking the 1.0-mile Vista Loop, which will lead you to three observation decks that overlook the Big Sioux River.

Many of the trails are heavily forested, and tree species found within the park include bur oak, boxelder, willow, cottonwood, basswood, green ash, hackberry, silver maple, and American elm. Be on the lookout for falcons, owls, hawks, and eagles.

One of three overlooks along the Vista Loop Trail

NEWTON HILLS STATE PARK

Named after William Newton, one of the first Euro-American settlers of the area, this 1,063-acre state park is a scenic destination for those who enjoy hiking, canoeing, fishing, swimming, and camping. Snowshoeing and cross-country skiing are popular in the winter months. The park is located in a heavily forested area along the Coteau des Prairies. Common trees include bur oak, hackberry, American elm, ironwood, basswood, and green ash. According to South Dakota Game, Fish and Parks, burial mounds and artifacts discovered here suggest that the Woodland culture inhabited the area between 300 BCE and 900 CE. Newton Hills State Park is home to the Woodland Trail, which was designated a National Recreation Trail in 1976. In addition to the Woodland Trail, the park also has miles of multi-use trails that can be used by hikers.

When visiting the park, make sure to climb the observation tower, which provides an overview of the area. Autumn is a perfect time to do this, when all the deciduous trees are yellow, orange, and red.

While hiking the trails at Newton Hills, be on the lookout for birds such as eastern towhees, blue-gray gnatcatchers, lark sparrows, and ruby-throated hummingbirds.

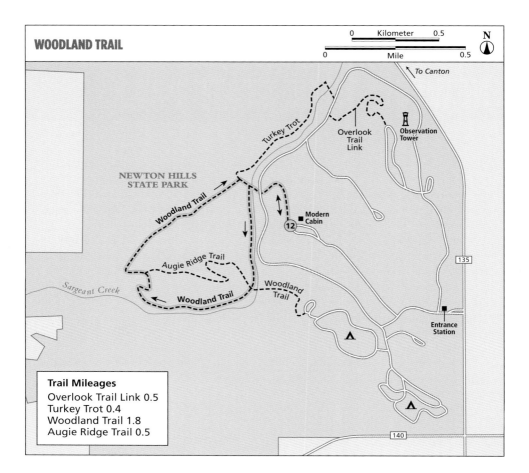

WOODLAND TRAIL

0   Kilometer   0.5

0   Mile   0.5

N

To Canton

Turkey Trot

Overlook
Trail
Link

Observation
Tower

NEWTON HILLS
STATE PARK

Woodland Trail

Modern
Cabin

12

135

Augie Ridge Trail

Sargeant Creek

Woodland Trail

Woodland
Trail

Entrance
Station

Trail Mileages
Overlook Trail Link 0.5
Turkey Trot 0.4
Woodland Trail 1.8
Augie Ridge Trail 0.5

140

12 WOODLAND TRAIL

A hike through a natural hardwood forest in southeastern South Dakota. The trail is open to foot traffic only and was designated a National Recreation Trail in 1976.

Start: At the trailhead in one of the park's day-use areas, near the modern cabin
Elevation gain: 1,318 to 1,490 feet
Distance: 1.8-mile lollipop
Difficulty: Moderate
Hiking time: 1 to 2 hours
Seasons: Best spring through fall
Fees and permits: Park entrance fee
Trail contact: Newton Hills State Park, 28767 482nd Ave., Canton, SD 57013; (605) 987-2263; https://gfp.sd.gov/parks/

Dog-friendly: Dogs must be on leash or under immediate control
Trail surface/conditions: Forested trail
Land status: Newton Hills State Park
Nearest town(s): Canton
Other trail users: Hikers only
Maps: State park map
Trailhead amenities: Available throughout park
Maximum grade: 10.1% for 0.3 mile (final ascent up to trailhead on return trip)

FINDING THE TRAILHEAD

From the city of Canton, head south on Lincoln CR 135 and follow it for about 7 miles. The entrance to the state park will be on your right (to the west). Once in the park, take the second right after the entrance station; the trailhead will be at the end of this road near the modern cabin (look for trailhead sign). GPS: N43 13.323' / W96 34.675'

THE HIKE

The Woodland Trail begins with a 160-foot descent through the forest to Sargeant Creek, named for Tom Sargeant, an early settler of the area. The trees along this descending slope have grown diagonally in a quest to reach more sunlight. At the bottom you will cross a park road and then the creek via a bridge (continue following signs for the Woodland Trail). The loop portion of the trail is reached after crossing Sargeant Creek; keep left (south) at the junction.

The trail follows the creek to the south, and at mile 0.6 there is a trail junction with the Augie Ridge Trail. *Option:* This 0.5-mile trail allows you to cut across the Woodland Trail loop (see map).

As you continue to follow the main Woodland Trail, the trail turns to the west and begins an ascent. It then reaches a high point, where there is a rest bench as well as the second junction with the Augie Ridge Trail.

From here, the trail descends back to the beginning of the loop, where you will cross back over the creek and park road, then make the 0.3-mile ascent back to the trailhead. *Option:* For a longer hike, begin on the other side of the park at the observation tower and descend to Sargeant Creek via the Overlook Trail. Across the creek, you will reach the junction with the Turkey Trot Trail, which will lead you in a southwesterly direction and eventually link up with the Woodland Trail.

Beams of sunlight stream through the dense forest during an early morning hike along the Woodland Trail

MILES AND DIRECTIONS

0.0 Start at the trailhead near the modern cabin (look for signage). The trail descends to Sargeant Creek.

0.3 Cross the park road and the bridge over the creek; keep left (south) at a junction and follow the Woodland Trail.

0.6 Junction with Augie Ridge Trail; go straight to remain on the Woodland Trail. From here, the trail begins its ascent. **Option:** This 0.5-mile trail allows you to cut across the Woodland Trail loop (see map).

1.1 The rest bench is reached at a high point, along with the second junction with the Augie Ridge Trail. Continue on the Woodland Trail.

1.5 You have reached the end of the loop; cross the bridge and park road to head back to the trailhead.

1.8 Arrive back at the trailhead.

UNION GROVE STATE PARK

This somewhat off-the-beaten-path state park located between the cities of Beresford and Vermillion offers the chance for hikers to spend some quiet time in nature. The 499-acre park consists of native woods and prairies that are home to a number of mammals as well as various species of birds such as blue jays, warblers, grosbeaks, cardinals, orioles, red-winged blackbirds, turkeys, and pheasants. In addition to the Brule Bottom Trail, the park also has more than 4 miles of multi-use trails (Mosey Meadow Multi-Use Trail System) that are open to horseback riding, biking, hiking, snowshoeing, and cross-country skiing.

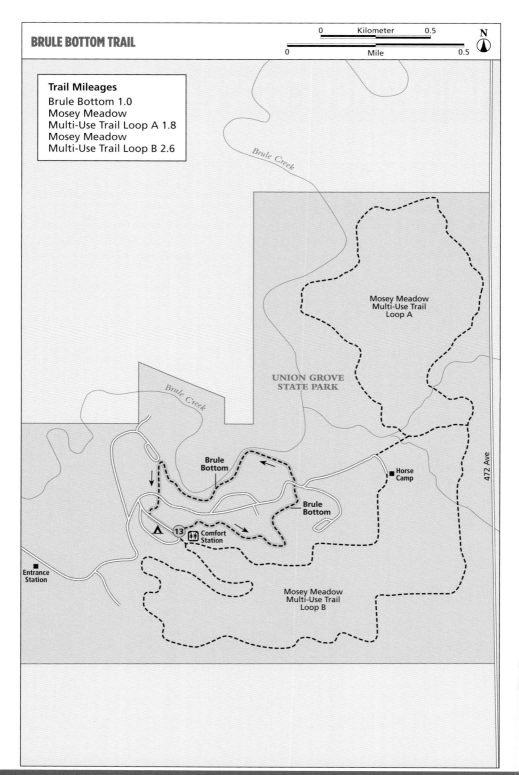

BRULE BOTTOM TRAIL

0 Kilometer 0.5
0 Mile 0.5

N

Trail Mileages
Brule Bottom 1.0
Mosey Meadow
Multi-Use Trail Loop A 1.8
Mosey Meadow
Multi-Use Trail Loop B 2.6

Brule Creek

Brule Creek

Mosey Meadow
Multi-Use Trail
Loop A

UNION GROVE
STATE PARK

472 Ave

Brule
Bottom

Horse
Camp

Brule
Bottom

Comfort
Station

13

Entrance
Station

Mosey Meadow
Multi-Use Trail
Loop B

13 BRULE BOTTOM TRAIL

A quiet hike through the dense woods of Union Grove State Park along Brule Creek.

Start: At the trailhead near the main campground's comfort station
Elevation gain: 1,305 to 1,421 feet
Distance: 1.0-mile loop
Difficulty: Easy
Hiking time: 30 minutes to 1 hour
Seasons: Best late spring through fall
Fees and permits: Park entrance fee
Trail contact: Union Grove State Park, 30828 471st Ave., Beresford, SD 57004; (605) 987-2263; https://gfp .sd.gov/parks/

Dog-friendly: Dogs must be on leash or under immediate control
Trail surface/conditions: Forested trail
Land status: Union Grove State Park
Nearest town(s): Beresford
Other trail users: Hikers only
Maps: State park map
Trailhead amenities: Available throughout park
Maximum grade: Negligible

FINDING THE TRAILHEAD

From the city of Beresford, take I-29 south for approximately 9 miles to exit 38. Turn left (east) onto 306th Street. After 0.6 mile, turn right (south) onto Union CR 1C/471st Avenue. After 2.3 miles, the state park entrance will be on your left (to the east). Follow signs to the park's main campground. The trailhead is near the comfort station. GPS: N42 55.269' / W96 46.736'

THE HIKE

According to South Dakota Game, Fish and Parks, there are more than 120 different species of trees that grow at Union Grove, including maple, bur oak, cottonwood, white cedar, ponderosa pine, and blue spruce.

This heavily forested hike begins at the southeast side of the campground and then gently descends to Brule Creek. The trail follows the creek in a westerly direction, reaches a picnic area, and then ascends back to the northeast side of the campground. The hike back to the trailhead, via the road in the campground, is less than 0.1 mile.

MILES AND DIRECTIONS

0.0   Start at the trailhead near the main campground's comfort station.

0.2   Reach a trail split; keep right (southeast).

0.3   Reach another trail split; keep left (northeast).

0.4   Cross the park road and remain on the Brule Bottom Trail.

0.9   At the picnic area, keep left (south) and ascend to the campground.

1.0   Arrive back at the trailhead.

Dense forest along the Brule Bottom Trail

MISSOURI RIVER

The Missouri River TRAVEL SOUTH DAKOTA

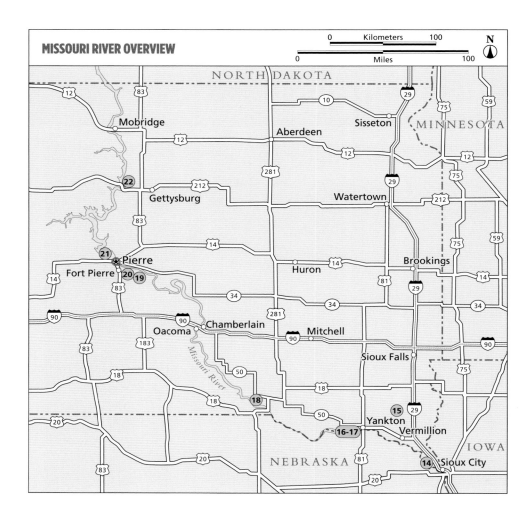

MISSOURI RIVER OVERVIEW

Kilometers
0   100

Miles
0   100

N

NORTH DAKOTA

MINNESOTA

Mobridge

Sisseton

Aberdeen

Gettysburg

Watertown

Pierre
Fort Pierre

Huron

Brookings

Oacoma
Chamberlain

Mitchell

Sioux Falls

Missouri River

Yankton
Vermillion

IOWA

NEBRASKA

Sioux City

ADAMS HOMESTEAD AND NATURE PRESERVE

Encompassing 1,500 acres along the Missouri River in the southeastern corner of South Dakota, the Adams Homestead and Nature Preserve is a great place to immerse yourself in nature while learning about the area's history. Stephen Searls Adams homesteaded this land in the early 1870s. His land was donated to the state by his granddaughters in 1984, and eventually became part of South Dakota's state park system in 1997. According to South Dakota Game, Fish and Parks, Stephen's granddaughters, Mary and Maud, "envisioned the area as a place where people, particularly youth, could enjoy the land and learn more about the natural world surrounding them." The preserve features prairies, lakes, groves of trees, and the Missouri River. While exploring the trails, be on the lookout for a variety of wildlife, as many mammals, reptiles, insects, birds, and amphibians live in this unique place. Also, plan to stop in to the visitor center museum to learn more about the area. The park is also a great place for a bike ride.

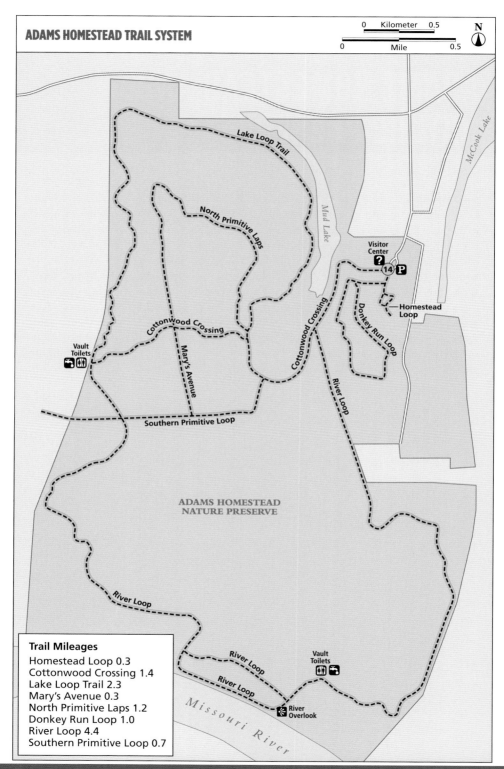

ADAMS HOMESTEAD TRAIL SYSTEM

0   Kilometer   0.5

0   Mile   0.5

N

McCook Lake

Lake Loop Trail

North Primitive Laps

Mud Lake

Visitor Center

14 P

Homestead Loop

Donkey Run Loop

Cottonwood Crossing

Cottonwood Crossing

Mary's Avenue

Vault Toilets

Southern Primitive Loop

River Loop

ADAMS HOMESTEAD
NATURE PRESERVE

River Loop

Vault Toilets

River Loop

River Loop

River Overlook

Missouri River

Trail Mileages

Homestead Loop 0.3
Cottonwood Crossing 1.4
Lake Loop Trail 2.3
Mary's Avenue 0.3
North Primitive Laps 1.2
Donkey Run Loop 1.0
River Loop 4.4
Southern Primitive Loop 0.7

14 ADAMS HOMESTEAD TRAIL SYSTEM

A series of trails that lead hikers through the area's history, prairies, forests, and to overlooks of the Missouri River.

Start: At the preserve's visitor center
Elevation gain: 1,096 to 1,141 feet
Distance: 11.6 miles of trails
Difficulty: Easy
Hiking time: Anywhere from 30 minutes to a full day
Seasons: All
Fees and permits: No fees or permits required
Trail contact: Adams Homestead and Nature Preserve, 272 Westshore Dr., McCook Lake, SD 57049; (605) 232-0873; https://gfp.sd.gov/parks/

Dog-friendly: Dogs must be on leash or under immediate control
Trail surface/conditions: Crushed limestone, mowed grass
Land status: Adams Homestead and Nature Preserve
Nearest town(s): North Sioux City
Other trail users: Mountain bikers, cross-country skiers, snowshoers
Maps: State park map
Trailhead amenities: Available at visitor center
Maximum grade: Negligible

FINDING THE TRAILHEAD

From North Sioux City, take exit 4 off I-29 and proceed west on Northshore Drive for about 1 mile. Turn left (south) onto Westshore Drive and follow signs to the preserve. GPS: N42 32.327' / W96 31.689'

THE HIKE

With so many trail options that make seemingly endless loops, it is easy to spend an entire day at the Adams Homestead and Nature Preserve.

Just south of the visitor center is the homestead itself, and short trails lead you around to all the historic buildings, including structures that were moved to the site and restored, such as the Stavanger Lutheran Church and the Lamont Country School. Children will enjoy visiting the homestead's barnyard to see the sheep, geese, and horses.

If you want to see the Missouri River, hike or bike on the River Loop Trail to the overlook south of the visitor center. Large cottonwood trees can be found along the Cottonwood Crossing Trail. And Mud Lake can be viewed from the Lake Loop Trail.

While at the preserve, be on the lookout for birds such as pied-billed grebes, northern pintails, whip-poor-wills, and blackpoll warblers.

The Missouri River as seen from the River Loop Trail

Visit the barnyard area at the homestead to see a variety of animals

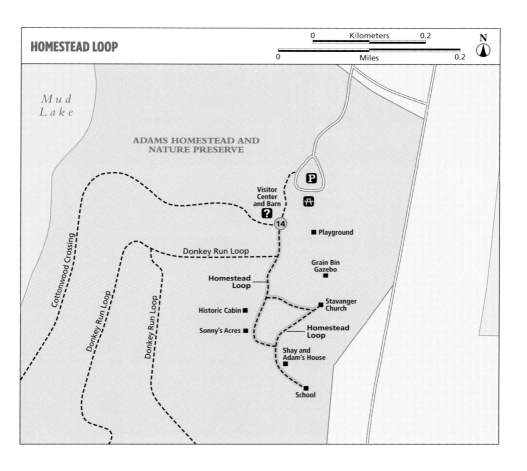

HOMESTEAD LOOP

0   Kilometers   0.2

0   Miles   0.2

N

Mud
Lake

ADAMS HOMESTEAD AND
NATURE PRESERVE

Visitor
Center
and Barn

🅿

⛺

❓

14

Playground

Cottonwood Crossing

Donkey Run Loop

Grain Bin
Gazebo

Homestead
Loop

Historic Cabin ■

Donkey Run Loop

Donkey Run Loop

Stavanger
Church

Sonny's Acres ■

Homestead
Loop

Shay and
Adam's House
■

School

SPIRIT MOUND HISTORIC PRAIRIE

On August 25, 1804, members of the Lewis and Clark Expedition (Corps of Discovery) visited Spirit Mound, a prominent natural landmark located to the north of the Missouri River near the present-day city of Vermillion. According to South Dakota Game, Fish and Parks, Spirit Mound is one of the "very few places where a person can stand today and know that Lewis and Clark stood in the same exact location."

Spirit Mound is what geologists refer to as a *roche moutonèe*, a knob made of bedrock that was not leveled flat by the last Pleistocene glacier some 13,000 years ago. Although other hills exist in the area, Spirit Mound is visually striking and when driving to it, can be seen for miles.

Traditional Native American stories told of the "hill of little people," and that Spirit Mound was a "place of the Devils." Lewis and Clark heard these stories from members of the Yankton, Omaha, and Oto tribes and decided that they would trek 9 miles overland from the Missouri River to the hill themselves.

The day before the hike, Clark wrote in his journal:

> *Capt Lewis and my Self Concluded to visit a High Hill Situated in an emence Plain three Leagues N. 20° W. from the mouth of White Stone river, this hill appear to be of a Conic form and by all the different Nations in this quater is Supposed to be a place of Deavels ors that they are in human form with remarkable large heads and about 18 inches high; that they are very watchfull and ar armed with Sharp arrows with which they can kill at a great distance; they are said to kill all persons who are so hardy as to attemp to approach the hill; they state that tradition informs them that many indians have suffered by these little people and among others that three Maha men fell a sacrefice to their murceyless fury not meany years since – so much do the Mahas Souix Ottoes and other neibhbouring nations believe this fable that no consideration is sufficient to induce them to approach this hill.*

Lewis and Clark, along with eleven other men, set out for Spirit Mound on August 25, apparently an extremely hot day. The expedition's dog, Seaman, had to be sent back to the river due to the heat. Once to the top of the hill, Lewis and Clark did not report seeing any spirits, but did observe almost 1,000 bison roaming the surrounding prairie. Clark noted:

> *from the top of this Mound we beheld a most butifull landscape; Numerous herds of buffalow were Seen feeding in various directions, the Plain to North N.W & N E extends without interuption as far as Can be Seen . . .*

As you walk to the top of Spirit Mound, imagine what the surrounding area would have looked like hundreds and thousands of years ago. And as always, when visiting, please be respectful of this important cultural site.

For more hiking in the Vermillion area, visit the 34-acre Clay County Park, located southwest of the city along the Missouri River.

—Lewis and Clark journal excerpts taken from public domain sources

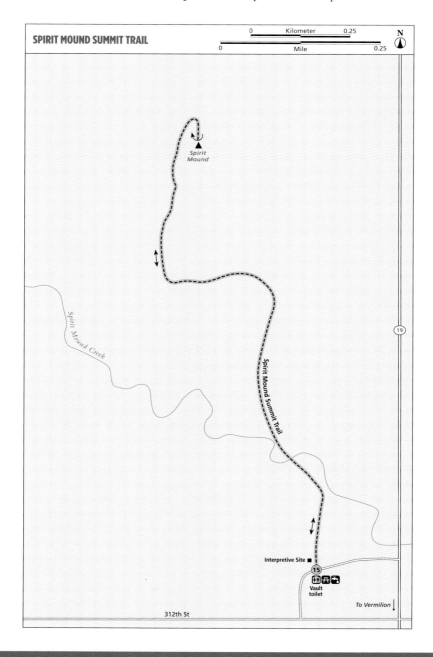

15 SPIRIT MOUND SUMMIT TRAIL

A short hike up to the top of a unique geological and historical feature on the prairies of southeastern South Dakota. The trail was designated a National Recreation Trail in 2004.

Start: At the Spirit Mound trailhead parking lot off SD 19
Elevation gain: 1,177 to 1,301 feet
Distance: 1.4 miles out and back
Difficulty: Moderate
Hiking time: 30 minutes to 1 hour
Seasons: Best spring through fall
Fees and permits: No fees or permits required
Trail contact: Spirit Mound Historic Prairie, 31148 SD Hwy. 19, Vermillion, SD 57069; (605) 987-2263; https://gfp.sd.gov/parks/

Dog-friendly: Dogs must be on leash or under immediate control
Trail surface/conditions: Crushed rock
Land status: Spirit Mound Historic Prairie
Nearest town(s): Vermillion
Other trail users: Hikers only
Maps: State park map
Trailhead amenities: Vault toilet, picnic tables
Maximum grade: 3.4% for 0.7 mile

FINDING THE TRAILHEAD

From the city of Vermillion, take SD 19 north for 5 miles to the trailhead parking lot, which will be on the left (to the west; look for signage). GPS: N42 52.052' / W96 57.362'

THE HIKE

Park staff remind hikers to please stay on the designated trail and not cut through areas of prairie restoration while hiking to Spirit Mound.

An information kiosk at the trailhead as well as several interpretive panels along the trail explain the area's geology, history, and ecology.

On clear days, those who venture to the top of Spirit Mound can see as far away as the Nebraska Bluffs (south), the Big Sioux River (southeast), and the James River (west).

While hiking through the prairie grasses, watch for birds such as Le Conte's sparrows, blue grosbeaks, upland sandpipers, bobolinks, and brown thrashers.

MILES AND DIRECTIONS

0.0 Start at the trailhead off SD 19, hiking north.

0.7 Reach the summit; retrace your steps back to the trailhead. Do not cut through the prairie on undesignated trails.

1.4 Arrive back at the trailhead.

Spirit Mound

LEWIS AND CLARK RECREATION AREA

This recreation area near the city of Yankton is one of the most popular in South Dakota's state park system. The area is located on the north shore of Lewis and Clark Lake, a 31,400-acre reservoir that was created by damming the Missouri River near Gavins Point. The park's location along the Missouri River makes it a popular destination for boating, canoeing, kayaking, paddleboarding, swimming, and fishing. Trails within the Lewis and Clark Recreation Area include the Chalk Bluffs Multi-Use Trail System, Gavins Point Nature Trail, and a bicycle/pedestrian trail that connects all the campgrounds and even has a spur into the city of Yankton itself.

GAVINS POINT NATURE TRAIL; CHALK BLUFFS LOOP

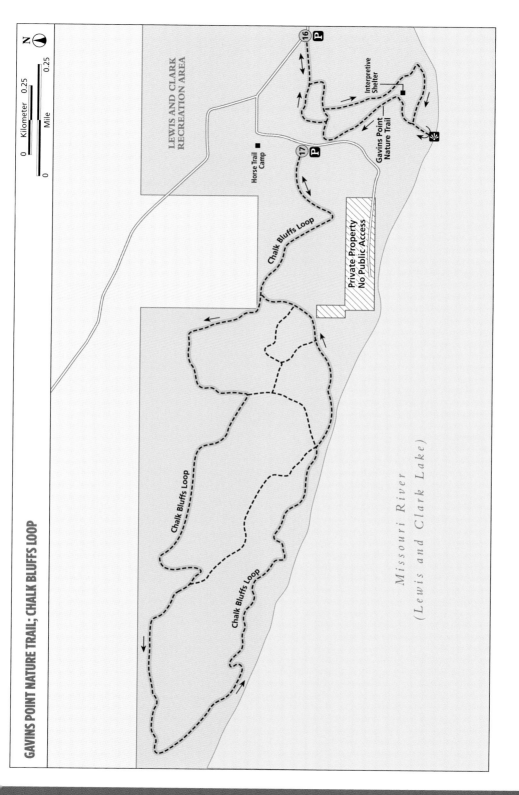

N

Kilometer
0   0.25

0   0.25
Mile

LEWIS AND CLARK
RECREATION AREA

Interpretive
Shelter

Gavins Point
Nature Trail

Horse Trail
Camp

Chalk Bluffs Loop

Chalk Bluffs Loop

Chalk Bluffs Loop

Chalk Bluffs Loop

Private Property
No Public Access

Missouri River
(Lewis and Clark Lake)

16 GAVINS POINT NATURE TRAIL

A short interpretive hike that leads to a scenic overlook of Lewis and Clark Lake.

Start: At the trailhead near the gazebo on the western side of the recreation area
Elevation gain: 1,200 to 1,311 feet
Distance: 1.2-mile lollipop
Difficulty: Easy to moderate
Hiking time: 30 minutes to 1 hour
Seasons: Best spring through fall
Fees and permits: Park entrance fee
Trail contact: Lewis and Clark Recreation Area, 43349 SD Hwy. 52, Yankton, SD 57078; (605) 668-2985; https://gfp.sd.gov/parks/

Dog-friendly: Dogs must be on leash or under immediate control
Trail surface/conditions: Forested trail, wood chips, boardwalk
Land status: Lewis and Clark State Recreation Area
Nearest town(s): Yankton
Other trail users: Hikers only
Maps: State park map
Trailhead amenities: Available throughout park
Maximum grade: Negligible

FINDING THE TRAILHEAD

From the city of Yankton, head west on SD 52 to the western entrance of Lewis and Clark Recreation Area, on your left (to the south). Proceed on Gavins Point Road until you see signage for the nature trail's parking lot (north of the boat ramp). GPS: N42 51.610' / W97 33.013'

THE HIKE

This hike, although moderate in some parts, can be a fun outing for families.

The trail winds through woods and meadows on its way to a scenic overlook. An interpretive shelter at the trail's highest point includes information on the Missouri River, Native American history, and the Lewis and Clark Expedition (Corps of Discovery).

Be on the lookout for deer and turkeys while hiking. Also be watching for birds such as American woodcocks, black-billed magpies, Bonaparte's gulls, and bald eagles.

MILES AND DIRECTIONS

0.0 Start at the trailhead parking lot off Gavins Point Road.

0.1 Reach the start of the loop; keep left (south; clockwise) and cross a wooden bridge.

0.2 Trail junction; keep left (south) to continue the loop.

0.6 A very short trail, on your left (southwest), leads up to a scenic overlook. After returning from the overlook, proceed straight (in a northeasterly direction) to hike up to the interpretive shelter.

0.7 You have reached the interpretive shelter. From here, the trail begins to descend.

0.9 Keep left (north) at a trail junction and cross a second wooden bridge.

1.1 Reach the end of the loop and head back to the trailhead parking lot.

1.2 Arrive back at the trailhead.

Gavins Point Nature Trail is suitable for the entire family

17 CHALK BLUFFS LOOP

A strenuous hike or bike ride along the Chalk Bluffs.
See map on page 105.

Start: At the Gavins Point Day-Use Area on the western side of the recreation area
Elevation gain: 1,215 to 1,431 feet
Distance: 3.6-mile lollipop
Difficulty: Strenuous
Hiking time: 2 to 3 hours
Seasons: Best spring through fall
Fees and permits: Park entrance fee
Trail contact: Lewis and Clark Recreation Area, 43349 SD Hwy. 52, Yankton, SD 57078; (605) 668-2985; https://gfp.sd.gov/parks/

Dog-friendly: Dogs must be on leash or under immediate control
Trail surface/conditions: Forested trail
Land status: Lewis and Clark State Recreation Area
Nearest town(s): Yankton
Other trail users: Mountain bikers, horseback riders
Maps: State park map
Trailhead amenities: Available throughout park
Maximum grade: 8.5% for 0.3 mile

FINDING THE TRAILHEAD

From the city of Yankton, head west on SD 52 to the western entrance of Lewis and Clark Recreation Area, on your left (to the south). Proceed on Gavins Point Road and follow signs for the day-use area and horse camp. The trailhead is located just to the south of the horse camp. GPS: N42 51.627' / W97 33.306'

THE HIKE

The Chalk Bluffs Multi-Use Trail System provides hikers with many opportunities to get out and explore via a series of loop trails that traverse up and down the hills of South Dakota's chalk bluffs. The route described here has you hiking the perimeter of the trail system, which leads through dense forests, along creek beds, and up to scenic views of the Missouri River (Lewis and Clark Lake). The trail is open to hikers, mountain bikers, and horseback riders. If biking, you may have to walk your bike up and down some of the steeper hills.

The chalk bluffs consist of the Niobrara Formation, which is made up of fossil shells that were deposited here by an ancient sea.

MILES AND DIRECTIONS

0.0 Start at the trailhead parking just south of the horse camp and follow the main trail. This beginning section of trail rises 135 feet over 0.3 mile.

0.3 Trail junction; keep right (northwest) to begin the loop portion of the hike.

0.7 Trail junction; keep right (northwest) to continue the loop.

1.4 Trail junction; keep right (northwest).

1.9 You have reached the westernmost point of the loop; keep left (southeast) to continue on the loop.

View of the Missouri River (Lewis and Clark Lake) from the Chalk Bluffs

2.8   Trail junction; keep right (southeast).

3.1   Trail junction; proceed straight (northeast).

3.2   Trail junction; proceed straight (northeast).

3.3   Reach the end of the loop; turn right (east/southeast) to hike back to the trailhead parking lot.

3.6   Arrive back at the trailhead.

PEASE CREEK RECREATION AREA

Pease Creek Recreation Area is located on the east side of the Missouri River (Lake Francis Case) in south-central South Dakota. The park is a great place to hike, bike, horseback ride, camp, swim, and fish. The trail system is well marked with waymarking signs along the way. The creek is named for F. David Pease, who settled in the area in 1857.

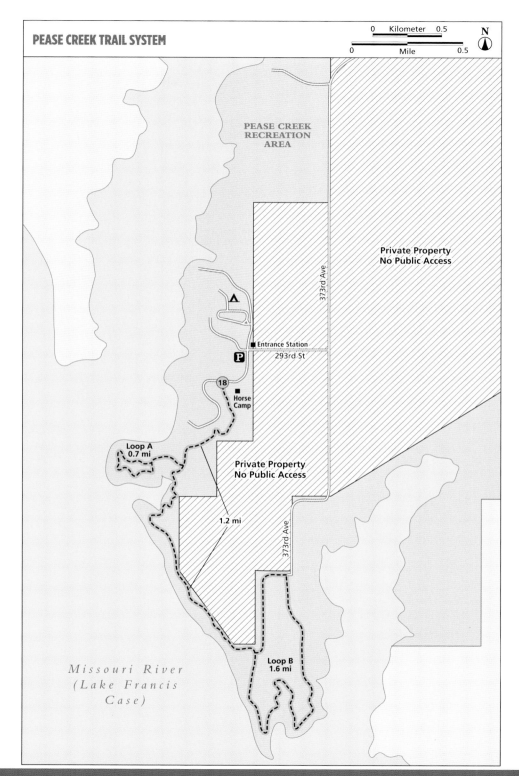

PEASE CREEK TRAIL SYSTEM

0   Kilometer   0.5

0   Mile   0.5

N

PEASE CREEK RECREATION AREA

Private Property
No Public Access

373rd Ave

■ Entrance Station

293rd St

P

18

■ Horse Camp

**Loop A
0.7 mi**

Private Property
No Public Access

1.2 mi

373rd Ave

*Missouri River
(Lake Francis
Case)*

**Loop B
1.6 mi**

18 PEASE CREEK TRAIL SYSTEM

A hike along the Missouri River bluffs in south-central South Dakota.

Start: At the trailhead in the park's equestrian camp
Elevation gain: 1,383 to 1,484 feet
Distance: 3.5 miles of trails including 2 loops
Difficulty: Moderate
Hiking time: 1 to 3 hours
Seasons: Best spring through fall
Fees and permits: Park entrance fee
Trail contact: Pease Creek Recreation Area, 37270 293rd St., Geddes, SD 57342; (605) 487-7046; https://gfp .sd.gov/parks/

Dog-friendly: Dogs must be on leash or under immediate control
Trail surface/conditions: Dirt path, mowed grass
Land status: Pease Creek State Recreation Area
Nearest town(s): Geddes, Lake Andes
Other trail users: Horseback riders, mountain bikers
Maps: State park map
Trailhead amenities: Available throughout park
Maximum grade: Varies; numerous ups and downs, yet none too difficult

FINDING THE TRAILHEAD

From the town of Geddes, take SD 50 south for approximately 6 miles to the junction with SD 1804. Proceed south on SD 1804 and follow signs to Pease Creek. At the park's entrance station, turn left (south) on a gravel road to the equestrian camp, which will be on the left. The trailhead is on the southern side of the camp; look for signage. GPS: N43 08.251' / W98 44.009'

THE HIKE

The Pease Creek Trail System is composed of 3.5 miles of trails that lead hikers through woods and prairies and up to the top of the Missouri River bluffs for sweeping overlooks of the area. With two separate loops, you can choose your own adventure; study the map for more details.

The trail begins on the southern side of the park's equestrian camp. There is a spot for a couple of vehicles to park near the trailhead. If that is full, there is a larger, gravel parking area near the entrance station that can also be used as a trailhead (you would have to walk along the road to the equestrian camp).

There are two optional loops, marked Loop A and B on the map. Both loops are very scenic and lead to overlooks of the Missouri River (Lake Francis Case). Loop A is 0.7 mile long; Loop B is 1.6 miles in length.

The trails are open to hiking, mountain biking, horseback riding, and in the winter, cross-country skiing and snowshoeing.

Check yourself for ticks after hiking here in the summer.

View of the Missouri River (Lake Francis Case) from the trails at Pease Creek Recreation Area

FARM ISLAND RECREATION AREA

Farm Island is an island in the Missouri River (Lake Sharpe) and is located southeast of the city of Pierre, South Dakota's state capital. A long time ago, fur traders and trappers named this piece of land "Farm Island" due to the fact that they planted crops there in the island's fertile soil.

In 1804, while traveling up the Missouri River, the Lewis and Clark Expedition (Corps of Discovery) stopped on the island to pick up some meat from an elk that the men had hunted and killed.

The recreation area is a popular destination for hiking, swimming, camping, fishing, bicycling, and bird-watching. The Farm Island Trail System received its National Recreation Trail designation in 1981.

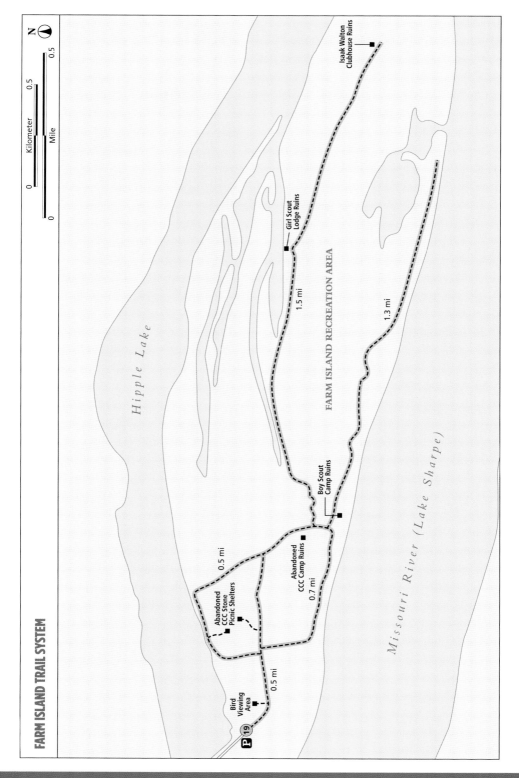

FARM ISLAND TRAIL SYSTEM

N

Kilometer
0   0.5

Mile
0   0.5

Hipple Lake

FARM ISLAND RECREATION AREA

Missouri River (Lake Sharpe)

Isaak Walton
Clubhouse Ruins

Girl Scout
Lodge Ruins

1.5 mi

1.3 mi

Boy Scout
Camp Ruins

Abandoned
CCC Stone
Picnic Shelters

0.5 mi

Abandoned
CCC Camp Ruins

0.7 mi

0.5 mi

Bird
Viewing
Area

P 19

19 FARM ISLAND TRAIL SYSTEM

A trail system that explores an island in the Missouri River, leading hikers to historic sites and wonderful views of the river.

Start: At the parking lot across the causeway (follow signs)
Elevation gain: 1,385 to 1,455 feet
Distance: 4.5 miles of trails
Difficulty: Easy
Hiking time: 30 minutes to a full day
Seasons: Best spring through fall
Fees and permits: Park entrance fee
Trail contact: Farm Island Recreation Area, 1301 Farm Island Rd., Pierre, SD 57501; (605) 773-2885; https://gfp .sd.gov/parks/

Dog-friendly: Check https://gfp .sd.gov/parks/ for current pet restrictions within state nature areas
Trail surface/conditions: Sand, gravel, mowed grass, forested trail
Land status: Farm Island State Recreation Area
Nearest town(s): Pierre
Other trail users: Mountain bikers
Maps: State park map
Trailhead amenities: Available throughout park
Maximum grade: Negligible

FINDING THE TRAILHEAD

From the city of Pierre, travel east on SD 34 until you reach Farm Island Road. Turn right (south) and travel 1 mile to the trailhead parking lot (follow signs). GPS: N44 20.241' / W100 16.480'

THE HIKE

In the summer of 1933, the Civilian Conservation Corps (CCC) set up camp on Farm Island and began working on a causeway to connect the island to the mainland. The 850-foot causeway was completed in the fall of 1934, and visitors to the island today can still see the remnants of the CCC's presence on the island. The island's trails lead hikers through the woods to abandoned CCC stone picnic shelters as well as the site of their camp. In addition to the CCC ruins, trails also lead to the remains of an old Boy Scout camp, a Girl Scout lodge, and an Izaak Walton Clubhouse.

Farm Island is a great place to hike or mountain bike. Birders should be on the lookout for bald eagles, willow flycatchers, pine siskins, and green herons. Make sure to bring your insect repellent and check yourself for ticks after spending time on the island.

View of the Missouri River (Lake Sharpe) on the south side of the island

CCC ruins on Farm Island

LAFRAMBOISE ISLAND NATURE AREA

Named after Joseph LaFramboise, an early fur trapper in the region, LaFramboise Island Nature Area is located on an island in the Missouri River near Pierre, South Dakota's state capital. The sandbar island is connected to the mainland via a causeway. The Lewis and Clark Expedition (Corps of Discovery) passed by the island on their way up the Missouri River in 1804. The expedition members saw many bison and elk on the island and named it "Good Humored Island," reflecting their positive mood that day. Although the island is no longer home to bison or elk, visitors today can see deer and rabbits, as well as a variety of bird species such as bald eagles, wild turkeys, great blue herons, and least terns.

The island is a good place for mountain biking. Make sure to bring insect repellent and check yourself for ticks after spending time on the island.

Pierre is a very bike-friendly city. There are bike trails that link from LaFramboise Island to the Oahe Downstream Recreation Area (page 122) to the north and the Farm Island Recreation Area (page 114) to the southeast. Maps are available at the Pierre Area Chamber of Commerce.

LAFRAMBOISE ISLAND TRAIL SYSTEM

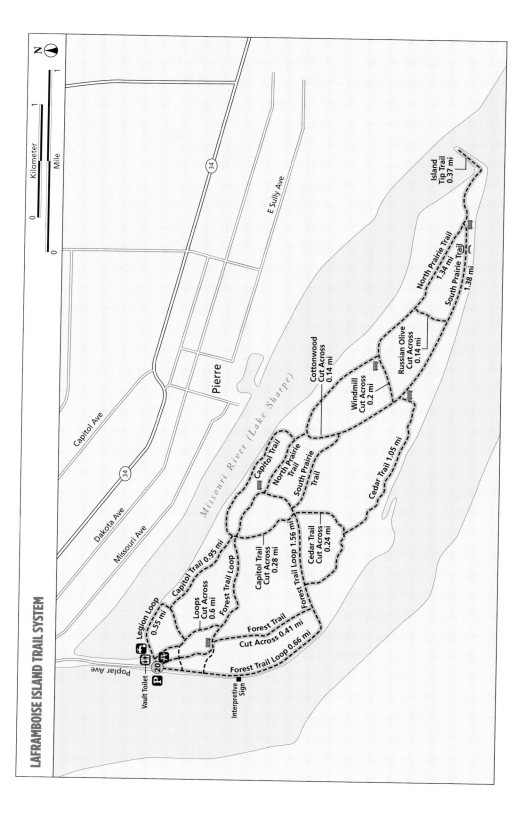

20 LAFRAMBOISE ISLAND TRAIL SYSTEM

A series of trails that explore LaFramboise Island in the Missouri River near Pierre. The trail system received its National Recreation Trail designation in 1981.

Start: At the trailhead parking lot at the end of Poplar Avenue in Pierre
Elevation gain: 1,437 to 1,454 feet
Distance: Approximately 9.5 miles of trails
Difficulty: Easy
Hiking time: 30 minutes to a full day
Seasons: All
Fees and permits: No fees or permits required
Trail contact: LaFramboise Island Nature Area (managed by Farm Island Recreation Area), 1301 Farm Island Rd., Pierre, SD 57501; (605) 773-2885; https://gfp.sd.gov/parks/

Dog-friendly: Check https://gfp.sd.gov/parks/ for current pet restrictions within state nature areas
Trail surface/conditions: Sand, mowed grass, forested trail
Land status: LaFramboise Island Nature Area
Nearest town(s): Pierre
Other trail users: Mountain bikers, cross-country skiers, snowshoers
Maps: State park map
Trailhead amenities: Toilets, picnic tables
Maximum grade: Negligible

FINDING THE TRAILHEAD

In the city of Pierre, take Poplar Avenue south off US 14 and follow the road across the causeway to the trailhead parking lot on the island (look for signage). GPS: N44 21.661' / W100 21.765'

THE HIKE

LaFramboise Island is a peaceful place for a short walk, an all-day hike, or a half-day bike ride. The trail system is well marked and well mapped. If on a mountain bike, there are several single-track trails that are fun to explore while maneuvering through the woods.

Interpretive signs along the trails explain the history of the island and its habitat. On some of the trails you can see the state capitol's rotunda rising above the tree line. The island is filled with cottonwood, eastern red cedar, green ash, Rocky Mountain juniper, and Russian olive trees. Birders should be on the lookout for bay-breasted warblers, purple finches, Caspian terns, and great blue herons.

Hiking and biking are particularly easy due to almost zero elevation change. Make sure to bring your insect repellent and check yourself for ticks after spending time on the island.

LaFramboise Island is a great place for a hike or bike ride JOHN MITCHELL

View of the Missouri River from the island's southeastern tip

OAHE DOWNSTREAM RECREATION AREA

This recreation area is located immediately downstream of the Oahe Dam on the Missouri River, which creates Lake Oahe. The US Army Corps of Engineers began construction of the dam in 1948, and it started generating electricity in 1962. Ownership of the 933-acre recreation area was transferred from the Corps to the State of South Dakota in 2002. The park is a great place to watch for bald eagles.

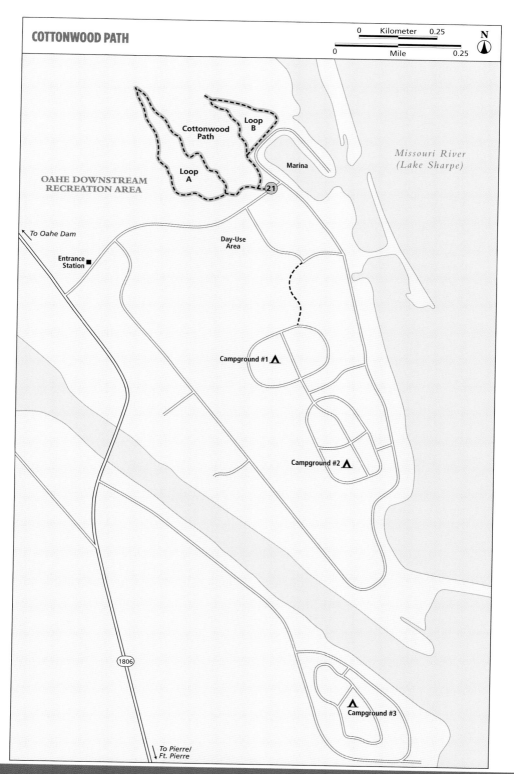

COTTONWOOD PATH

0   Kilometer   0.25
0   Mile   0.25

N

Cottonwood Path

Loop B

Loop A

Missouri River
(Lake Sharpe)

Marina

OAHE DOWNSTREAM
RECREATION AREA

21

To Oahe Dam

Day-Use
Area

Entrance
Station

Campground #1

Campground #2

1806

Campground #3

To Pierre/
Ft. Pierre

21 COTTONWOOD PATH

A National Recreation Trail that leads hikers through towering cottonwood trees at Oahe Downstream Recreation Area along the Missouri River north of Fort Pierre. A portion of the trail is accessible.

Start: At the trailhead's interpretive shelter on the north side of the park's day-use area (look for signage)
Elevation gain: 1,426 to 1,452 feet
Distance: 1.5-mile figure eight
Difficulty: Easy
Hiking time: 30 minutes to 1 hour
Seasons: Best spring through fall
Fees and permits: Park entrance fee
Trail contact: Oahe Downstream Recreation Area, 20439 Marina Loop Rd., Fort Pierre, SD 57532; (605) 223-7722; https://gfp.sd.gov/parks/

Dog-friendly: Dogs must be on leash or under immediate control
Trail surface/conditions: Sand, forested path, paved trail
Land status: Oahe Downstream State Recreation Area
Nearest town(s): Fort Pierre, Pierre
Other trail users: Bikers
Maps: State park map
Trailhead amenities: Available throughout park
Maximum grade: Negligible

FINDING THE TRAILHEAD

From the city of Fort Pierre, take SD 1806 north for 4 miles. Turn right onto Power House Road and follow it for less than 1 mile to the entrance of the recreation area, on your right. Past the entrance station, there is a large parking lot for the park's marina and day-use area. The Cottonwood Path begins to the north of the parking lot at the interpretive shelter (look for signage). GPS: N44 26.398' / W100 23.566'

THE HIKE

The Cottonwood Path was designated a National Recreation Trail in 1981 and, like the name suggests, leads hikers through towering cottonwood trees in the shadow of Oahe Dam. Make sure to be on the lookout for bald eagles. Other birds to watch for include geese, ducks, and terns.

The path makes a figure eight with two loops, marked Loop A and Loop B on the map. Both sections of trail begin at the interpretive shelter, which has information about Native American history, Missouri River steamboats, archaeology, and bald eagles. Loop A is a sandy, forested, 0.9-mile lollipop. Loop B is a paved, accessible, 0.6-mile lollipop.

Besides cottonwoods, other trees found along the trail include elm, American sycamore, green ash, honey locust, Russian olive, and basswood.

Large trees along the Cottonwood Path

WEST WHITLOCK RECREATION AREA

West Whitlock Recreation Area is located on the eastern side of the Missouri River (Lake Oahe) in north-central South Dakota. This area was once the home of the Arikara and Mandan peoples, who lived in earthen lodges and farmed the lands of the upper Missouri. In early October 1804, the Lewis and Clark Expedition (Corps of Discovery) stopped in this area at an abandoned Arikara village.

The recreation area became a part of South Dakota's state park system in 1983. Whitlocks Crossing was the name of an old settlement in the area that operated a ferry across the river.

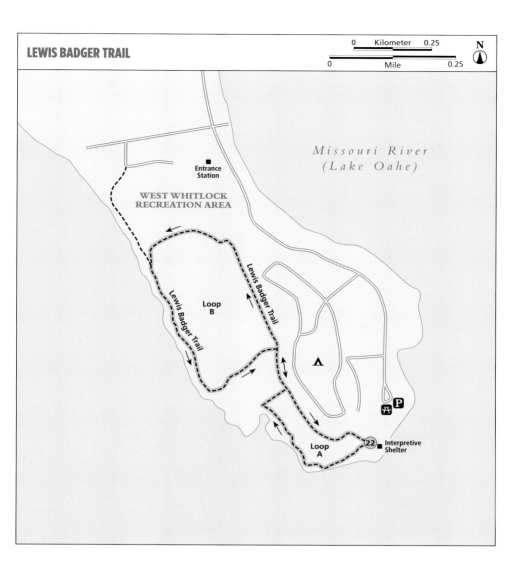

LEWIS BADGER TRAIL

0 Kilometer 0.25

0 Mile 0.25

N

Missouri River
(Lake Oahe)

Entrance Station

WEST WHITLOCK RECREATION AREA

Loop B

Lewis Badger Trail

Lewis Badger Trail

Loop A

22 Interpretive Shelter

22 LEWIS BADGER TRAIL

A hike along the eastern shore of the Missouri River (Lake Oahe) in north-central South Dakota.

Start: At the trailhead's interpretive shelter near the park's day-use area
Elevation gain: 1,615 to 1,637 feet
Distance: 1.7-mile figure eight
Difficulty: Easy
Hiking time: 30 minutes to 1 hour
Seasons: Best spring through fall
Fees and permits: Park entrance fee
Trail contact: West Whitlock Recreation Area; 16157 W. Whitlock, Ste. A, Gettysburg, SD 57442; (605) 765-9410; https://gfp.sd.gov/parks/

Dog-friendly: Dogs must be on leash or under immediate control
Trail surface/conditions: Sand, forested trail, mowed grass
Land status: West Whitlock State Recreation Area
Nearest town(s): Gettysburg
Other trail users: Hikers only
Maps: State park map
Trailhead amenities: Available throughout park
Maximum grade: Negligible

FINDING THE TRAILHEAD

From the town of Gettysburg, head west on US 212 for approximately 12 miles. Turn right (north) onto SD 1804. After about 4 miles, turn left onto West Whitlock Road and follow signs to the recreation area. The trail begins at the interpretive shelter near the park's day-use area. GPS: N45 02.384' / W100 15.575'

THE HIKE

Charles Lewis Badger cared for the trees that were planted at West Whitlock Recreation Area in the 1960s, and the trail here is named in his honor. While hiking on the trail, be on the lookout for sharp-tailed grouse, gulls, and a variety of songbirds.

The trail begins at the interpretive shelter located in an open, grassy area in the park's southeast corner. Interpretive panels thoroughly explain the history of the area. The trail contains two loops, marked Loop A and Loop B on the map, and can be hiked in several ways, but the description here has you hiking in a figure eight.

From the interpretive shelter, take the path to the left and follow the trail along the shoreline. It soon enters a shaded area with stands of tall trees. Around 0.35 mile, you will reach a trail junction; keep left (northwest) to continue on the connector trail to Loop B or, for a much shorter hike, turn right (southeast) to head back to the trailhead.

If continuing on the connector trail, Loop B is reached only 0.1 mile later. Continuing on Loop B, which is a 0.9-mile loop, the trail heads northwest through a shaded area before it begins to turn west and then southeast. This final section of Loop B parallels the shoreline again and is open with no shade. After hiking a total of 1.3 miles, you return to the connector trail and can make your way back to the trailhead.

MILES AND DIRECTIONS

0.0 Start at the trailhead's interpretive shelter in the park's day-use area, beginning on the left fork.

0.35 Trail junction; keep left (northwest) on the connector trail to Loop B. Alternatively, for a much shorter hike, you can turn right (southeast) and return to the trailhead.

0.45 Loop B is reached; proceed straight (northwest).

1.3 End of Loop B; turn right (south/southeast) on the connector trail.

1.4 Junction with Loop A; proceed straight (southeast) to hike back to the trailhead.

1.7 Arrive back at the trailhead.

View of the Missouri River from the Lewis Badger Trail

BADLANDS

Badlands National Park ANDREW PESCHONG

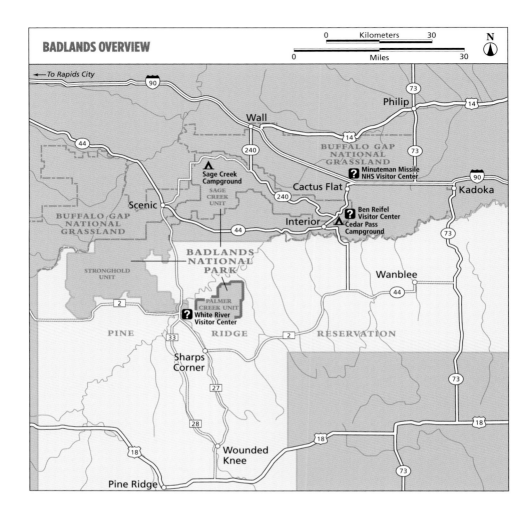

BADLANDS OVERVIEW

0 Kilometers 30

0 Miles 30

N

To Rapids City

90

73

Philip

14

Wall

14

240

BUFFALO GAP
NATIONAL
GRASSLAND

73

90

Minuteman Missile
NHS Visitor Center

Cactus Flat

Kadoka

44

Scenic

240

SAGE
CREEK
UNIT

Sage Creek
Campground

Ben Reifel
Visitor Center

Interior

Cedar Pass
Campground

73

BUFFALO GAP
NATIONAL
GRASSLAND

44

BADLANDS
NATIONAL
PARK

STRONGHOLD
UNIT

Wanblee

44

2

PALMER
CREEK UNIT

White River
Visitor Center

PINE

RIDGE

2

RESERVATION

33

73

Sharps
Corner

27

28

18

73

18

18

18

Wounded
Knee

73

Pine Ridge

BADLANDS NATIONAL PARK

The Lakota call the Badlands Mako Sica, which translates to "land that is bad." The French trappers who traveled the region in the early 1800s arrived at a similar designation, describing them as the mauvaises terres à traverser, or "bad lands to travel across."

Badlands geology began with the encroachment of oceans millions of years ago. Over eons, these waters deposited many sediments. Approximately 38 million years ago, ash from volcanic activity in what is now Colorado landed in much of the Great Plains and Black Hills region. This ash, mixed with other sediments from the Black Hills, was deposited throughout the area.

Streams and rivers flowed from the evolving mountains, carrying with them some of the sediments deposited by ancient seas. Eventually these sandstones, banded clays, and limestones were redeposited in what came to be known as the White River Badlands, named for one of the rivers that transported a portion of these materials. Erosional forces then acted on these soft sediments, creating some of the nation's most spectacular formations.

Badlands National Park encompasses 244,300 acres and preserves the largest protected mixed-grass prairie in the United States, with 64,250 acres of wilderness. The park was established in 1939 as a national monument and designated a national park in 1978. Plan a visit to the museum located inside the Ben Reifel Visitor Center to learn more about the natural history of South Dakota's badlands.

When hiking, remember that the badlands terrain is very fragile. Exercise caution and try to minimize damage by remaining on established paths. Pets of any kind are not allowed on the trails. Be on the lookout for bison and rattlesnakes. And carry lots of water, particularly in summer when hiking the longer trails. The Badlands contain no potable water; all water must be carried in. Bikes and motorized vehicles are allowed on paved roads only; they are off-limits on all of the park's trails as well as throughout the various wilderness areas. Expect high winds and brief but violent thunderstorms in the warmer months.

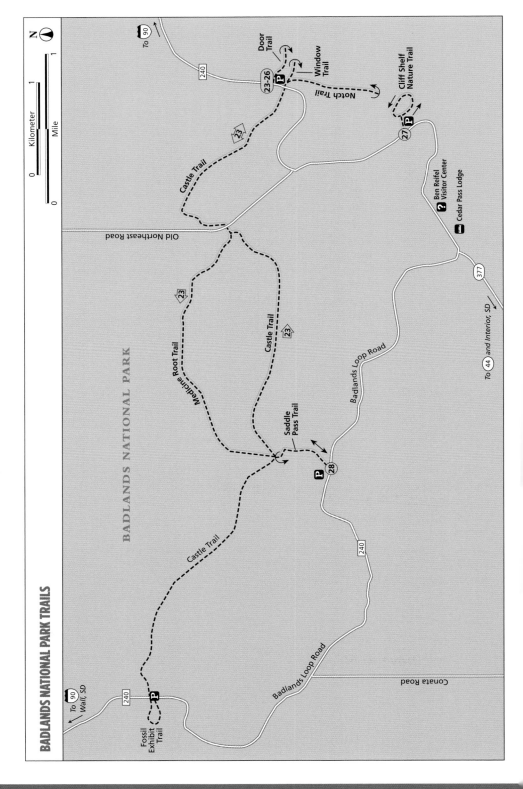

BADLANDS NATIONAL PARK TRAILS

South Dakota's badlands have always held a special place in my heart. I have spent countless hours wandering around the park, which has continually provided great inspiration for me. One misty, eerie day in particular still holds a place in my memory, and it led to my first published poem, printed in *South Dakota Magazine* as well as the literary journal *Oakwood*. I like to say this is "my only claim to poetry fame."

Badlands Solitaire

The wind blows through the grass
Yet I hear nothing

I have encountered wildlife
With a cold reception
This is their place
It belongs to them

Distant buffalo await my approach
They will be ready
The bird chirps
Breaking the unrelenting silence

Soft mist
Sun, grace us with your presence
I beg of you

Where am I?
I am not welcomed

The deer ran off with a scamper

I see everything
Yet I hear nothing.

23 CASTLE-MEDICINE ROOT LOOP

A lengthy loop hike that leads through South Dakota's badlands. This makes a great sunrise hike.

Start: At the Castle Trail trailhead across from the Door, Window, and Notch Trails
Elevation gain: 2,583 to 2,654 feet
Distance: 6.8-mile lollipop
Difficulty: Easy
Hiking time: 3 to 5 hours
Seasons: Best spring through fall
Fees and permits: Park entrance fee
Trail contact: Badlands National Park, 25216 Ben Reifel Rd., Interior,

SD 57750; (605) 433-5361; www.nps.gov/badl
Dog-friendly: Dogs not allowed
Trail surface/conditions: Dirt path
Land status: Badlands National Park
Nearest town(s): Wall, Interior
Other trail users: Hikers only
Maps: National Geographic/Trails Illustrated Topo Map No. 239; Badlands National Park brochure
Trailhead amenities: Vault toilets
Maximum grade: Negligible

FINDING THE TRAILHEAD

Take SD 240 (Badlands Loop Road) north from the Ben Reifel Visitor Center for approximately 2 miles to the trail's parking area on the right (east) side of the road. The trailhead is located across the road (to the west) from the Door, Window, and Notch Trails (look for signage). GPS: N43 45.675' / W101 55.672'

THE HIKE

The Castle-Medicine Root Loop is a flat, easy walk along a narrow dirt path through a grasslands area. As you walk along this plateau, grasslands sweep to the north while the jagged wall formations rise to the south. Other formations range from short, flat, sod-covered "tables" to lofty spires and "toadstools." The area surrounding the trail is covered with prickly pear cactus and prairie wildflowers. Watch out for sinkholes along the trails! Also be on the lookout for wildlife such as deer and coyotes.

You will begin on the Castle Trail (marked by red metal posts), hike to Old Northeast Road, and then continue on the Medicine Root Trail (marked by green metal posts). The Medicine Root Trail ends at the junction of the Saddle Pass and Castle Trails.

To complete the loop, take the Castle Trail (marked by signs) leading back to the east. The trail ambles along the base of interesting rock formations, once again reaches the Old Northeast Road, and then brings you back to the trailhead.

Watch your footing while on this trail. Sturdy hiking boots are recommended to hike through the badlands formations. The trail is relatively easy due to minimal elevation gain. Make sure to look for the metal posts that serve as trail markers.

MILES AND DIRECTIONS

0.0 Start at the eastern Castle Trail trailhead, across from the Door, Window, and Notch Trails parking lot.

1.4 Cross Old Northeast Road; keep right (northwest) on the Medicine Root Trail.

3.6 Junction with Castle and Saddle Pass Trails; turn left (east) on the Castle Trail. **Option:** For a much longer hike, you can head west for about 2.0 miles on the Castle Trail all the way to the Fossil Exhibit Trail (see Bonus Hikes and map for details).

5.4 The trail returns to Old Northeast Road to close the loop. Retrace your steps on the Castle Trail, heading in an easterly direction.

6.8 Arrive back at the trailhead.

Sunrise along the Medicine Root Trail on a cold autumn morning

Unique badlands formations along the Castle Trail

24 **DOOR TRAIL**

An interpretive walk through impressive badlands formations.

Start: At the northern end of the trailhead parking lot, 2 miles north of the visitor center
Elevation gain: 2,600 to 2,627 feet
Distance: 0.8 mile out and back
Difficulty: Easy to moderate
Hiking time: 30 minutes to 1 hour
Seasons: Best spring through fall
Fees and permits: Park entrance fee
Trail contact: Badlands National Park, 25216 Ben Reifel Rd., Interior, SD 57750; (605) 433-5361; www.nps.gov/badl

Dog-friendly: Dogs not allowed
Trail surface/conditions: Boardwalk, dirt path
Land status: Badlands National Park
Nearest town(s): Wall, Interior
Other trail users: Hikers only
Maps: National Geographic/Trails Illustrated Topo Map No. 239; Badlands National Park brochure
Trailhead amenities: Vault toilets
Maximum grade: Negligible

FINDING THE TRAILHEAD

 The Door Trail is located 2 miles north of the Ben Reifel Visitor Center on SD 240 (Badlands Loop Road). The trail begins at the northern end of the parking lot (look for trailhead signage). GPS: N43 45.813' / W101 55.600'

THE HIKE

The first segment of the Door Trail is accessible (via a boardwalk) and allows visitors to enter and pass through the "door," where some of the Badlands' most rugged terrain greets you. The remaining portion of the trail is rough but flat, and sturdy hiking boots are recommended. The terrain is fragile with many loose edges. Exercise caution. The trail is marked by yellow metal posts. Do not venture past the "End of Trail" sign.

MILES AND DIRECTIONS

0.0 Start at the north side of the trailhead parking lot, 2 miles north of the park's visitor center.

0.1 The accessible portion of the trail ends; turn right (south) and walk down steps to continue the hike.

0.4 Reach the "End of Trail" sign; turn around and retrace your steps.

0.8 Arrive back at the trailhead parking lot.

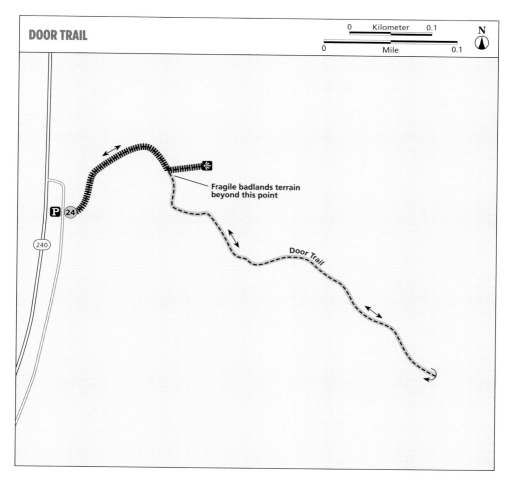

DOOR TRAIL

0   Kilometer   0.1

0   Mile   0.1

N

Fragile badlands terrain
beyond this point

Door Trail

240

"End of Trail" sign at the end of the Door Trail

25 WINDOW TRAIL

A short walk to a "window" that offers a fantastic overview of South Dakota's badlands.
See map on page 134.

Start: At the southern end of the trailhead parking lot, 2 miles north of the visitor center
Elevation gain: 2,633 to 2,643 feet
Distance: 0.2 mile out and back
Difficulty: Easy
Hiking time: About 15 minutes
Seasons: Best spring through fall
Fees and permits: Park entrance fee
Trail contact: Badlands National Park, 25216 Ben Reifel Rd., Interior,

SD 57750; (605) 433-5361; www.nps.gov/badl
Dog-friendly: Dogs not allowed
Trail surface/conditions: Boardwalk
Land status: Badlands National Park
Nearest town(s): Wall, Interior
Other trail users: Hikers only
Maps: National Geographic/Trails Illustrated Topo Map No. 239; Badlands National Park brochure
Trailhead amenities: Vault toilets
Maximum grade: Negligible

FINDING THE TRAILHEAD

The Window Trail is located 2 miles north of the Ben Reifel Visitor Center on SD 240 (Badlands Loop Road). The hike begins on the south side of the trailhead parking lot (look for trailhead signage). GPS: N43 45.639' / W101 55.660'

THE HIKE

The Window Trail is an easy walk to a natural "window" in the Badlands Wall. The trail is accessible via a boardwalk.

MILES AND DIRECTIONS

0.0 Start at the southern end of the trailhead parking lot, 2 miles north of the park's visitor center.

0.1 Reach the scenic overlook; turn around and retrace your steps.

0.2 Arrive back at the trailhead parking lot.

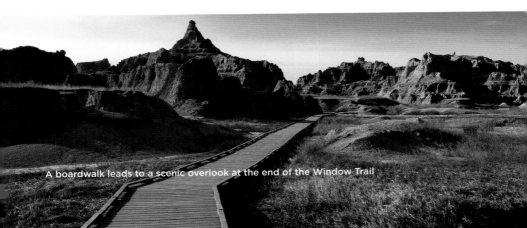

A boardwalk leads to a scenic overlook at the end of the Window Trail

26 **NOTCH TRAIL**

A hike through and then to the top of a canyon that ends at an overlook on top of a cliff.

Start: At the southern end of the trailhead parking lot, 2 miles north of the visitor center
Elevation gain: 2,662 to 2,790 feet
Distance: 1.4 miles out and back
Difficulty: Moderate
Hiking time: 1 to 2 hours
Seasons: Spring through fall
Fees and permits: Park entrance fee
Trail contact: Badlands National Park, 25216 Ben Reifel Rd., Interior, SD 57750; (605) 433-5361; www.nps.gov/badl

Dog-friendly: Dogs not allowed
Trail surface/conditions: Dirt path, ladder
Land status: Badlands National Park
Nearest town(s): Wall, Interior
Other trail users: Hikers only
Maps: National Geographic/Trails Illustrated Topo Map No. 239; Badlands National Park brochure
Trailhead amenities: Vault toilets
Maximum grade: An approximately 50-foot climb up a rope ladder

FINDING THE TRAILHEAD

The Notch Trail is located 2 miles north of the Ben Reifel Visitor Center on SD 240 (Badlands Loop Road). The trail begins at the southern end of the trailhead parking lot near the Window Trail (Hike 25). GPS: N43 45.605' / W101 55.691'

THE HIKE

For the first 0.3 mile, the Notch Trail meanders along a canyon floor around rocks and delicate prairie flowers. Then it reaches a fifty-six-rung rope ladder, which is cabled into the hill. If you are afraid of heights, this might be a good point to turn around and head back to the trailhead.

Upon climbing to the top of the ladder, you will follow the scuffed trail that winds around rock ledges above the canyon until it emerges and ends at the top of a cliff, providing a commanding overlook of the valley. Here, you stand on part of a cliff that collapsed long ago and formed the Cliff Shelf Nature Trail (Hike 27), lying directly below. From this point you can also see the park's campground and the town of Interior. Use caution, as this trail can be slippery when wet. Retrace your steps, descending the ladder this time, to return to the trailhead.

The trail is marked by dark metal posts with white tips.

MILES AND DIRECTIONS

0.0 Start at the southern end of the trailhead parking lot, 2 miles north of the park's visitor center. The trail begins at the southern end of the trailhead parking lot (look for signage).

0.3 Reach the rope ladder; carefully ascend to the rim of the canyon.

0.7 The trail ends at an overlook; retrace your steps to return to the trailhead.

1.4 Arrive back at the trailhead parking lot.

The rope ladder on the Notch Trail

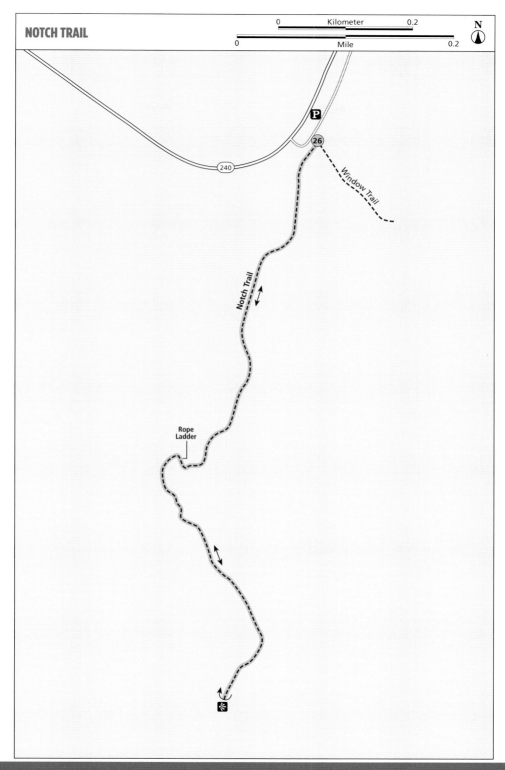

0   Kilometer   0.2

0   Mile   0.2

N

240

P

26

Window Trail

Notch Trail

Rope
Ladder

27 CLIFF SHELF NATURE TRAIL

An interpretive trail along an ancient cliff shelf that collapsed long ago from the imposing cliffs above.
See map on page 134.

Start: At the Cliff Shelf trailhead, 0.5 mile east of the visitor center
Elevation gain: 2,601 to 2,699 feet
Distance: 0.5-mile loop
Difficulty: Easy to moderate
Hiking time: About 30 minutes
Seasons: Best spring through fall
Fees and permits: Park entrance fee
Trail contact: Badlands National Park, 25216 Ben Reifel Rd., Interior, SD 57750; (605) 433-5361; www.nps.gov/badl

Dog-friendly: Dogs not allowed
Trail surface/conditions: Boardwalk, dirt path
Land status: Badlands National Park
Nearest town(s): Wall, Interior
Other trail users: Hikers only
Maps: National Geographic/Trails Illustrated Topo Map No. 239; Badlands National Park brochure
Trailhead amenities: None; available at nearby visitor center
Maximum grade: 6.4% for 0.2 mile

FINDING THE TRAILHEAD

The Cliff Shelf Nature Trail is accessed from a point 0.5 mile east of the Ben Reifel Visitor Center on SD 240 (Badlands Loop Road). The parking lot is small and not suitable for vehicles towing trailers or any other type of large vehicle such as an RV. GPS: N43 45.029' / W101 55.863'

THE HIKE

Fascinating natural history stories exist here at the collapsed Cliff Shelf, which fell many years ago due to underground moisture creating slumps and landslides. The geologic facts of the area are explained thoroughly by interpretive panels along the trail.

The trail undulates through a wooded prairie but is wide and has a stairway. A portion of the trail is accessible. The park has provided several rest benches along the walk, and you will be treated to wonderful views of the White River valley.

MILES AND DIRECTIONS

0.0 Start at the trailhead parking lot off SD 240, hiking counterclockwise.

0.2 Reach the trail's highest elevation.

0.5 Arrive back at the trailhead parking lot.

Steps near the high point of the Cliff Shelf Nature Trail JOHN MITCHELL

28 **SADDLE PASS TRAIL**

A short and steep trail through a pass. The trail is impassable after rains, and still slippery if at all wet.
See map on page 134.

Start: At the trailhead on the SD 240 (Badlands Loop Road), 2 miles west of the visitor center
Elevation gain: 2,422 to 2,651 feet
Distance: 0.7 mile out and back
Difficulty: Strenuous
Hiking time: About 45 minutes
Seasons: Best spring through fall
Fees and permits: Park entrance fee
Trail contact: Badlands National Park, 25216 Ben Reifel Rd., Interior, SD 57750; (605) 433-5361; www.nps.gov/badl

Dog-friendly: Dogs not allowed
Trail surface/conditions: Dirt path
Land status: Badlands National Park
Nearest town(s): Wall, Interior
Other trail users: Hikers only
Maps: National Geographic/Trails Illustrated Topo Map No. 239; Badlands National Park brochure
Trailhead amenities: None; available at nearby visitor center
Maximum grade: 14.5% for 0.3 mile

FINDING THE TRAILHEAD

The Saddle Pass Trail can be accessed from SD 240 (Badlands Loop Road), about 2 miles west of the Ben Reifel Visitor Center. The trailhead parking lot is on the north side of the road. GPS: N43 45.483' / W101 58.467'

THE HIKE

The Saddle Pass Trail (marked with blue metal posts) is a 200-foot elevation–gain scramble over unique badlands formations. Simultaneously, the trail provides grand vistas of the park, particularly at the summit. At times, especially when wet, the trail can be treacherous—the clay soil turns to "gumbo," which is very slippery and sticky.

At the summit the Saddle Pass Trail links with both the Castle Trail and the Medicine Root Trail (see map for more details). From here, you have the choice of descending the route you just climbed or linking with one of these two trails.

MILES AND DIRECTIONS

0.0 Start at the trailhead parking lot 2 miles west of the park's visitor center on SD 240.

0.35 The trail ends at the summit, with the option to continue hiking on the Castle or Medicine Root Trails. If not, carefully retrace your steps back down the hill.

0.7 Arrive back at the trailhead parking lot.

View from the top of the Saddle Pass Trail

BLACK HILLS

View of the central granite core of the Black Hills

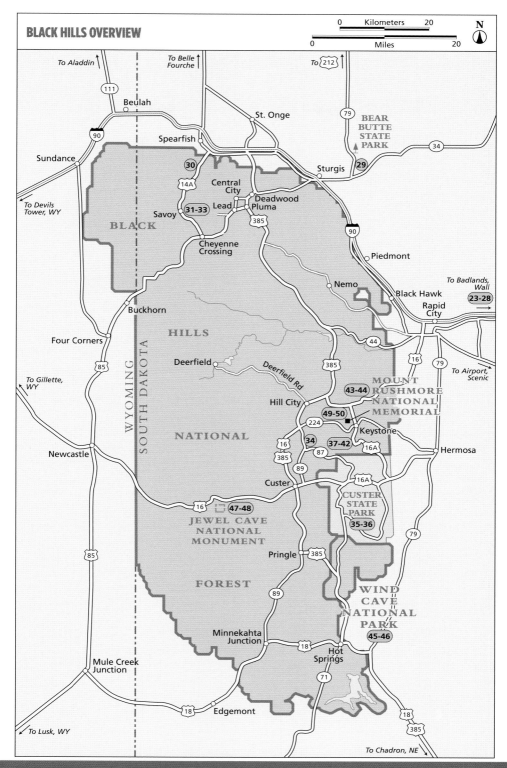

0 Kilometers 20

0 Miles 20

N

To Aladdin

To Belle
Fourche

To 212

111

Beulah

St. Onge

79

BEAR
BUTTE
STATE
PARK

90

Spearfish

Sundance

34

30

14A

Central
City

Sturgis

29

To Devils
Tower, WY

31-33

Savoy

Lead

Deadwood
Pluma

385

90

BLACK

Cheyenne
Crossing

Piedmont

Buckhorn

Nemo

Black Hawk

To Badlands,
Wall

Rapid
City

23-28

HILLS

Four Corners

85

Deerfield

Deerfield Rd

385

44

16

79

To Airport,
Scenic

To Gillette,
WY

WYOMING

SOUTH DAKOTA

NATIONAL

Hill City

43-44

MOUNT
RUSHMORE
NATIONAL
MEMORIAL

49-50

224

Keystone

Newcastle

16
385

34

87

37-42

16A

Hermosa

89

Custer

16A

85

16

47-48

JEWEL CAVE
NATIONAL
MONUMENT

CUSTER
STATE
PARK

35-36

79

Pringle

385

FOREST

89

WIND
CAVE
NATIONAL
PARK

45-46

Minnekahta
Junction

18

Hot
Springs

Mule Creek
Junction

71

18

Edgemont

18

385

To Lusk, WY

To Chadron, NE

BEAR BUTTE STATE PARK

We did not think of the great open plains, the beautiful rolling hills, and the winding streams with tangled growth, as wild. Earth was bountiful and we were surrounded with the blessings of the great Mystery.

—Luther Standing Bear, Lakota Nation

Bear Butte is not a butte at all, but a solidified intrusion of a certain type of igneous rock, formed in much the same way many other area mountains were sculpted, such as Crow Peak near Spearfish (Hike 30). Bear Butte is a laccolith made of rhyolite that was pushed through the surface by magma around 50 million years ago. The mountain is the eastern-most exposed igneous intrusion from the Tertiary period in the Black Hills.

Rising 1,200 feet above the plains, it is located just outside the northeast corner of the Black Hills, approximately 8 miles northeast of Sturgis, South Dakota, and is part of Bear Butte State Park.

In 1965 the mountain was designated a National Natural Landmark because of its exceptional value in illustrating a unique segment of the natural history of the United States. In 1973 Bear Butte was placed on the National Register of Historic Places because of its service as a beacon and its spiritual significance to Native American nations. The Cheyenne call the mountain Noavosse, meaning "Good Mountain," while the Lakota call it Mato Paha, or "Bear Mountain."

Native Americans have tied prayer flags and bundles in trees over the many years of their use of the landmark. Please do not disturb them. Observe off-limits signs and do not intrude on those who may be praying or meditating. Take only scenic photos and none of ceremonial objects.

In 1996 a massive fire ravaged much of Bear Butte, consuming about 90 percent of the ponderosa pine trees on the mountain. The effects of the fire will remain for many, many years, but the surrounding grasslands are rebounding quickly. The natural process of fire and its part in ecology is evidenced in a huge way, one that you will see as you hike.

The area around Bear Butte, especially by the lake, is a great place for bird-watching, so be on the lookout for mountain bluebirds, eagles, long-eared owls, and sharp-tailed grouse.

Pets of any kind are not allowed on the trails. Mountain biking is not permitted. Water is available at the park's education center during normal business hours and on the trail, a couple hundred feet from the trailhead.

Bear Butte as viewed from a section of the Centennial Trail

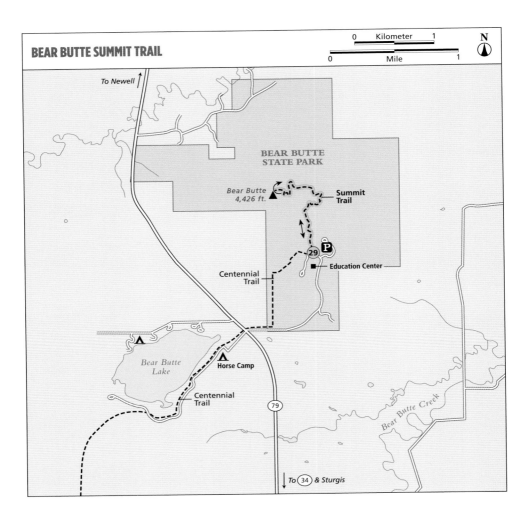

0   Kilometer   1

0   Mile   1

N

To Newell

BEAR BUTTE
STATE PARK

Bear Butte
4,426 ft.

Summit
Trail

P

29

Education Center

Centennial
Trail

Bear Butte
Lake

Horse Camp

Centennial
Trail

79

Bear Butte Creek

To 34 & Sturgis

29 BEAR BUTTE SUMMIT TRAIL

A beautiful, invigorating hike from the base to the peak of a sacred mountain. The trail, rising more than 1,000 feet in only 1.6 miles, winds through a burned pine forest area; many tree branches are draped with prayer flags and ceremonial objects. The trail was designated a National Recreation Trail in 1971.

Start: At the trailhead near the Bear Butte Education Center
Elevation gain: 3,378 to 4,426 feet
Distance: 3.2 miles out and back
Difficulty: Strenuous due to steep ascent over a short distance
Hiking time: 2 to 3 hours
Seasons: Best late spring through fall
Fees and permits: Park entrance fee
Trail contact: Bear Butte State Park, PO Box 688, Sturgis, SD 57785; (605) 347-5240; https://gfp.sd.gov/parks/

Dog-friendly: Dogs not allowed
Trail surface/conditions: Rocky path; limited shade
Land status: Bear Butte State Park
Nearest town(s): Sturgis
Other trail users: Hikers only
Maps: State park map
Trailhead amenities: Toilets, picnic tables, visitor center
Maximum grade: 13% for 1.6 miles

FINDING THE TRAILHEAD

From the town of Sturgis, take SD 34 east for 5 miles to SD 79. Go north on SD 79 for 3 miles to the sign on the right for Bear Butte State Park. The trailhead is located near the Bear Butte Education Center, a 1-mile drive up the road from the turn off SD 79. GPS: N44 28.099' / W103 25.249'

THE HIKE

Reminder: Pets of any kind are not allowed on the trail. Mountain biking is also not permitted. Summers are extremely hot, and the trail has little to no available shade. Hiking during extreme heat conditions is not recommended. Also, the trail may be very icy during winter months.

Begin the hike on the Summit Trail, which is well marked at the trailhead at the education center parking lot. This is also part of the Black Hills' Centennial Trail. The dirt path is wide and ascends through stands of pine, crossing talus slopes and offering numerous switchbacks.

Follow the Summit Trail for 0.8 mile to the point where the trail swings left (west) and reaches the second rest bench. At this point you can continue up to the peak on the Summit Trail or descend back to the parking lot, making a shorter hike of almost 2.0 miles. However, it is well worth the effort to continue to the peak.

The Summit Trail continues winding around the cliffs, with numerous switchbacks. Do not cut and make new trails between switchbacks. Where washouts might occur, park managers have placed log steps. The third rest bench is reached after 1.3 miles, where you find yourself standing above an enormous talus slope. You reach the summit 0.3 mile later and are rewarded with commanding 360–degree views of the lake, bison herd, ponds, farms, and cattle; the Black Hills looming to the southwest; and the Badlands stretching to the east.

From the peak, retrace the hike along the Summit Trail and descend back to the trailhead. While on your way back down from the peak, please remember again not to cut switchbacks.

MILES AND DIRECTIONS

- **0.0** Start on the Summit Trail, hiking north from the trailhead parking lot.
- **0.35** You will reach a trail split; the trail to your left (west) has a more gentle ascent. The trail to your right (north/northeast) rises abruptly but shaves off about 0.1 mile from the hike (this trail might be easier to take when descending from the mountain).
- **0.5** Reach the first rest bench.
- **0.8** Continue left (west) on the Summit Trail near the second rest bench.
- **1.3** Arrive at the third rest bench; the summit is near.
- **1.6** Reach the summit of Bear Butte and the observation deck. Retrace your route.
- **3.2** Arrive back at the trailhead parking lot.

Bear Butte as viewed from a section of the Centennial Trail

Be prepared when hiking to the summit of Bear Butte.

The trail rises for more than 1,000 feet in only 1.6 miles. With limited shade along the trail, hiking during hot summer days can be unforgiving.

After autumn snowstorms, in winter, and well into spring, MICROspikes are recommended. When looking at Bear Butte from the trailhead parking lot, you are looking at the sunny side of the mountain. The Summit Trail swings around to the shady back side of the mountain, and the trail is usually covered with ice or packed-down snow.

One time on a warm day in January, I was getting ready to hike Bear Butte when a state park official stopped me at the trailhead parking lot and asked if I had any ice spikes. I showed him my MICROspikes and he said, "Wow, those are good." I would not recommend anything else. Slipping and falling off the back side of Bear Butte would cause major injury or death, as it is very steep, and the mountain is covered with sharp rocks.

SPEARFISH AREA

The Spearfish Canyon area is so special that a scenic byway winds almost 20 miles through the canyon walls and tree-covered slopes, providing a tour of unparalleled beauty.

The Spearfish Canyon formations began to take shape approximately 62 million years ago. Geologically, three types of rocks dominate the canyon's walls and can be clearly viewed in several places. The top (the thickest and youngest) layer is Pahasapa Limestone and is usually gray. The middle layer is Englewood Limestone and consists of reddish hues. The bottom is brown and layered, and referred to as Deadwood Shale. Vertically formed dark gray rocks called phonolite intrusions may also be seen in some areas. Bridal Veil Falls drops from a formation that is a prime example of this condition.

Botanically, four distinctly different vegetative regions thrive in the canyon. The area is a meeting place for plants, trees, and bushes from the Great Plains, the Rocky Mountains, and the eastern deciduous and northern forests.

This area is known for its waterfalls. There are two short trails near Savoy that lead to waterfalls, which are described in this section. Additionally, Bridal Veil Falls is located 7 miles north of Savoy on US 14A and can be viewed from the road.

While driving through Spearfish Canyon, watch for birds such as red-tailed hawks, canyon wrens, ruby-crowned kinglets, American dippers, and plumbeous vireos.

For longer hikes in the Spearfish area, consider hiking on the Old Baldy, Little Spearfish, Rimrock, or Big Hill Trails. For complete trail descriptions, see *Hiking the Black Hills Country*, also by FalconGuides.

Sunrise in Spearfish Canyon

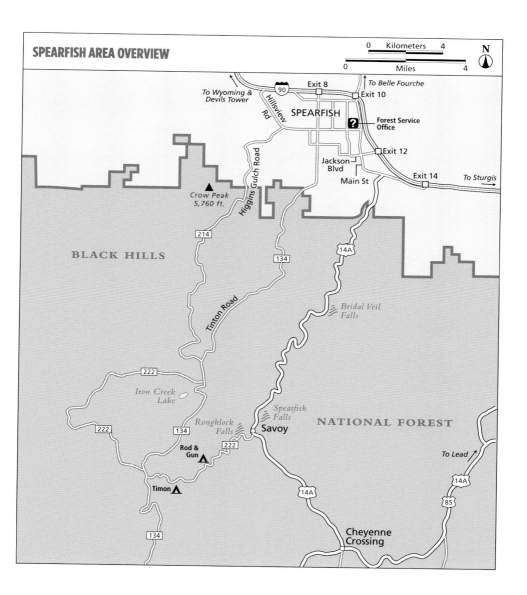

SPEARFISH AREA OVERVIEW

0 Kilometers 4
0 Miles 4

N

To Belle Fourche
Exit 8
Exit 10
To Wyoming & Devils Tower
90
Hillsview Rd
SPEARFISH
Forest Service Office
Exit 12
Jackson Blvd
Main St
Exit 14
To Sturgis
Crow Peak 5,760 ft.
Higgins Gulch Road
BLACK HILLS
214
134
14A
Bridal Veil Falls
Tinton Road
222
Iron Creek Lake
222
134
Roughlock Falls
Spearfish Falls
Savoy
NATIONAL FOREST
Rod & Gun
222
To Lead
Timon
14A
14A
85
134
Cheyenne Crossing

Bridal Veil Falls

30 **CROW PEAK**

A day hike winding upward through pine forests to fantastic panoramas at the summit. The trail is steep, with a total elevation gain of more than 1,500 feet. Carry an ample supply of drinking water.

Start: At the trailhead parking lot on Higgins Gulch Road (FR 214)
Elevation gain: 4,241 to 5,760 feet
Distance: 6.6 miles out and back
Difficulty: Strenuous due to continuous incline
Hiking time: 3 to 4 hours
Seasons: Best late spring through fall
Fees and permits: No fees or permits required
Trail contact: Northern Hills Ranger District, 2014 N. Main St., Spearfish, SD 57783; (605) 642-4622; www.fs.usda.gov/bhnf

Dog-friendly: Leashed dogs permitted
Trail surface/conditions: Rocky, forested trail
Land status: Black Hills National Forest
Nearest town(s): Spearfish
Other trail users: Horseback riders, mountain bikers
Maps: Black Hills National Forest Map; BHNF Crow Peak Trail Map No. 64; National Geographic/Trails Illustrated Topo Map No. 751
Trailhead amenities: None
Maximum grade: 8.8% for 3.3 miles

FINDING THE TRAILHEAD

The trailhead is about 6 miles southwest of Spearfish off I-90 via exit 8. From exit 8, proceed south on McGuigan Road for about 1 mile to Hillsview Road. Turn right onto Hillsview Road, and after 1 mile, turn left on Higgins Gulch Road (FR 214) and follow it for 3.9 miles to the trailhead and a large parking area on the right. GPS: N44 28.020' / W103 56.874'

THE HIKE

Crow Peak is a popular hike. The trail winds up to the mountaintop, providing sweeping vistas at the summit. Crow Peak is so named because of a battle once fought here between the Crow and Sioux Nations. Appropriately, the mountain's name in the Lakota language, Paha Karitukateyapi, translates to "the place where the Sioux killed the Crow."

Crow Peak is a laccolithic igneous intrusion and was formed in the same manner as Bear Butte (page 150) and several other peaks in the area. Between 61 and 39 million years ago, molten magma broke through the limestone and sedimentary layers, which then cooled to form the hard, igneous rock. Erosion and washing away of sedimentary deposits continue to re-form the hills in the area.

The trail begins in Higgins Gulch amid ponderosa pine woods and much new growth of native bushes and bur oak. The 3.3 miles up the peak is moderate in some places, strenuous in others. The route heads west on the southern side of the mountain and climbs ever upward. The trail is well traveled and well marked.

At about 1.9 miles you will encounter a junction. Here you might want to take the 1.0-mile round-trip Beaver Ridge Spur Trail to the southwest. If not, continue in a northerly direction toward the summit.

As the trail nears the top, the forest thins and the path becomes rockier. Simultaneously the trail offers the promise of spectacular views ahead—and the peak lives up to that promise.

Lookout, Spearfish, and Terry Peaks as well as Bear Butte and other high points appear in the east. The plains of eastern Montana and the Bearlodge Mountains of Wyoming lie to the west, with Warren Peak sometimes visible. The Black Hills National Forest Trail No. 64 brochure provides a sketch map of all the major mountain peaks you can see from the top of Crow Peak. This brochure can be obtained from the Black Hills National Forest district office in Spearfish.

MILES AND DIRECTIONS

0.0 Start at the trailhead parking lot on Higgins Gulch Road.

1.9 The Beaver Ridge Spur Trail comes in from the left (west). Option: This out-and-back trail will add 1.0 mile to the hike if you elect to take it.

3.3 You have reached the summit; backtrack from Crow Peak.

6.6 Arrive back at the trailhead.

View of the northern Black Hills from atop Crow Peak

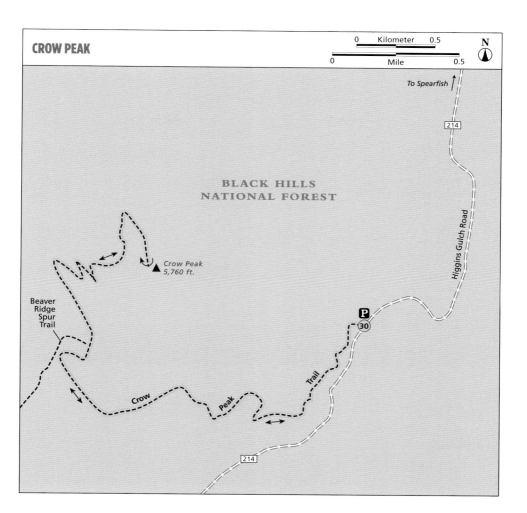

CROW PEAK

BLACK HILLS
NATIONAL FOREST

Crow Peak
5,760 ft.

Beaver
Ridge
Spur
Trail

Crow Peak Trail

Higgins Gulch Road

To Spearfish

214

214

P 30

0   Kilometer   0.5

0   Mile   0.5

N

31 **ROUGHLOCK FALLS**

An easy, scenic trail leading to Roughlock Falls.

Start: At the trailhead parking lot behind the Spearfish Canyon Lodge
Elevation gain: 5,002 to 5,114 feet
Distance: 2.0 miles out and back
Difficulty: Easy
Hiking time: 1 to 2 hours
Seasons: All
Fees and permits: No fees or permits required
Trail contact: South Dakota Game, Fish and Parks, 523 E. Capitol Ave., Pierre, SD 57501; (605) 584-3896; https://gfp.sd.gov/parks/

Dog-friendly: Leashed dogs permitted
Trail surface/conditions: Forested trail
Land status: Spearfish Canyon Nature Area
Nearest town(s): Spearfish
Other trail users: Hikers only
Maps: Black Hills National Forest Map; National Geographic/Trails Illustrated Topo Map No. 751
Trailhead amenities: Vault toilet
Maximum grade: Negligible

FINDING THE TRAILHEAD

The trailhead parking lot (gravel) is behind the Spearfish Canyon Lodge in Savoy, 13 miles south of Spearfish on US 14A (Spearfish Canyon Scenic Byway). **Note:** The paved parking lot immediately adjacent to the Spearfish Canyon Lodge is for registered guests only. GPS: N44 21.025' / W103 55.940'

THE HIKE

This easy, popular trail takes you alongside Little Spearfish Creek until it reaches Roughlock Falls. Once at the falls, there are viewing areas, picnic tables, and vault toilets. In winter, packed snow along the trail can be slippery; watch your footing.

MILES AND DIRECTIONS

0.0   Start at the trailhead from the gravel parking lot behind Spearfish Canyon Lodge.

1.0   You have reached Roughlock Falls; take some time to explore all the different viewing areas. Retrace your steps to return to the trailhead.

2.0   Arrive back at the trailhead.

Roughlock Falls BRITTANY KAHL

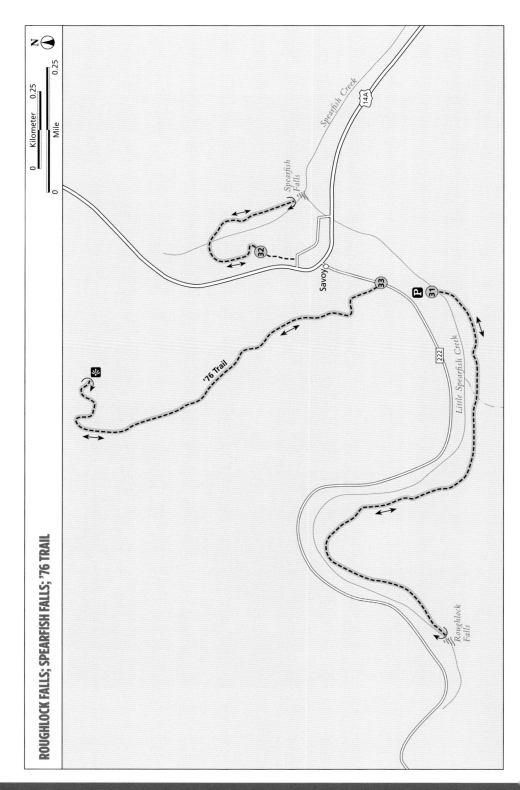

32 SPEARFISH FALLS

A short hike to Spearfish Falls in the depths of Spearfish Canyon. See map on page 164.

Start: At the trailhead parking lot behind the Spearfish Canyon Lodge
Elevation gain: 4,902 to 4,939 feet
Distance: 0.6 mile out and back
Difficulty: Easy
Hiking time: 30 minutes to 1 hour
Seasons: Best late spring through fall
Fees and permits: No fees or permits required
Trail contact: South Dakota Game, Fish and Parks, 523 E. Capitol Ave., Pierre, SD 57501; (605) 584-3896; https://gfp.sd.gov/parks/

Dog-friendly: Leashed dogs permitted
Trail surface/conditions: Forested trail; can be icy into late spring
Land status: Spearfish Canyon Nature Area
Nearest town(s): Spearfish
Other trail users: Hikers only
Maps: State park map
Trailhead amenities: Vault toilet
Maximum grade: Negligible

FINDING THE TRAILHEAD

The trailhead parking lot (gravel) is behind the Spearfish Canyon Lodge in Savoy, 13 miles south of Spearfish on US 14A (Spearfish Canyon Scenic Byway). **Note:** Recently, signs that read "Restaurant Parking Only" have been placed in the paved parking lot near the trailhead. To be courteous, parking at the same trailhead as Roughlock Falls (Hike 31) is recommended. The Spearfish Falls Trail begins on the north side of the restaurant. GPS: N44 21.231' / W103 55.870'

THE HIKE

This forested, scenic trail leads you down into the depths of Spearfish Canyon to Spearfish Falls. The waterfall is reached after a 0.3-mile hike and has rest benches and viewing areas.

MILES AND DIRECTIONS

0.0   Start at the trailhead across from Spearfish Canyon Lodge and on the north side of the restaurant.

0.3   You have reached Spearfish Falls. Retrace your steps to the trailhead.

0.6   Arrive back at the trailhead.

Spearfish Falls BRITTANY KAHL

33 '76 TRAIL

A strenuous but "well-worth-it" hike to the rim of Spearfish Canyon, offering spectacular views.
See map on page 164.

Start: At the trailhead parking lot behind the Spearfish Canyon Lodge
Elevation gain: 5,044 to 5,639 feet
Distance: 1.4 miles out and back
Difficulty: Strenuous due to continuous incline
Hiking time: 30 minutes to 1 hour
Seasons: Best late spring through early fall
Fees and permits: No fees or permits required
Trail contact: Northern Hills Ranger District, 2014 N. Main St., Spearfish, SD 57783; (605) 642-4622; www.fs.usda.gov/bhnf

Dog-friendly: Leashed dogs permitted
Trail surface/conditions: Rocky, forested trail
Land status: Black Hills National Forest
Nearest town(s): Spearfish
Other trail users: Hikers only
Maps: Black Hills National Forest Map; National Geographic/Trails Illustrated Map No. 751
Trailhead amenities: Vault toilet
Maximum grade: 16.1% for 0.7 mile

FINDING THE TRAILHEAD

The trailhead parking lot (gravel) is behind the Spearfish Canyon Lodge in Savoy, 13 miles south of Spearfish on US 14A (Spearfish Canyon Scenic Byway). **Note:** The paved parking lot immediately adjacent to the Spearfish Canyon Lodge is for registered guests only. You will have to park at the trailhead for Roughlock Falls (Hike 31) and walk across FR 222, as the trail begins on the north side of the road (look for the trailhead sign). GPS: N44 21.085' / W103 55.933'

THE HIKE

This hike is very strenuous but well worth the effort. Bringing small children along on this hike is not recommended. You will gain almost 600 feet of elevation in only 0.7 mile.

Beginning the hike at the trailhead on the north side of FR 222 opposite from Spearfish Canyon Lodge, follow the trail ever upward to the rim of Spearfish Canyon. Signs placed along the trail that read "Steep Climb Ahead" and "Loose Footing" warn trail users about its difficulty. If you do not think you can make it to the top, it might be best to turn around.

Once you reach the trail's highest point, you are treated to a panoramic view of Spearfish Canyon and the northern Black Hills. The viewpoint area is enclosed by a chain-link fence with a sign that reads "Do Not Go Beyond This Point; No Climbing." If not heeded, one misstep could be fatal.

MILES AND DIRECTIONS

0.0   Start at the trailhead on the north side of FR 222 opposite Spearfish Canyon Lodge.

0.7 You have reached the trail's overlook and highest point. Carefully retrace your steps down the canyon.

1.4 Arrive back at the trailhead.

View of Spearfish Canyon at the end of the '76 Trail

Autumn is a great time to hike the '76 Trail

CUSTER STATE PARK

In 1919, land that once had been a state game preserve officially became Custer State Park. Today the park contains 71,000 acres consisting of unique rock formations, grasslands, and forests of ponderosa pine, bur oak, and white spruce. As a wildlife preserve, the park has large bison herds and is also home to elk, deer, burros, bighorn sheep, and mountain goats. Custer State Park is one of the largest state parks in the nation.

When hiking in the park, always be aware of the possibility of bison encounters. Never approach bison. A cow with her calf in the spring represents a threat, as do animals of both sexes during the mating season. Also be on the lookout for rattlesnakes and check yourself for ticks after hiking through tall grass. Watch out for poison ivy near creeks.

Custer State Park is a special place. In an article written for the South Dakota School of Mines and Technology in 1926, C. C. O'Harra and J. P. Connolly explained:

> The value of Custer State Park as a recreation center is based primarily on its geology. The geology controls in large measure the intricate topography, and the topography in turn is influential in regulating the details of climate and distribution of plant and animal life, and it gives character everywhere to the scenic beauty so pronounced throughout the area.

This is still true today. From the southeastern corner near the buffalo corrals to the Cathedral Spires in the northwestern corner, you can explore the almost full succession of Black Hills geology dating from 2.2 billion to 30 million years ago.

To become acquainted with the park, it may be helpful to drive all three of the scenic roads provided to visitors. The vistas are incredible, and for those planning to hike, the drives provide a good overview of trail locations. The drives take longer than the mileages indicate because the roads are slow and winding. The Needles Highway is 14 miles long and curves its way around magnificent granite formations. The Iron Mountain Road is 17 miles in length, with pigtail bridges and tunnels carved through the granite rock. This road leads from Custer State Park to Mount Rushmore National Memorial near Keystone. Be aware that portions of the Needles Highway close and the Iron Mountain Road often closes during the winter season. Also, these two roads both include tunnels, so it is important to know the height and width of your vehicle. The 18-mile Wildlife Loop Road shows another side of the park—its rolling prairie grasslands and their magnificent display of wildlife.

A South Dakota State Park Pass is required to visit Custer State Park. For the most current fees, inquire at the visitor center or park entrance stations.

Note: At the time of publication, Custer State Park was in the process of developing a master plan for the Sylvan Lake area in an effort to reduce congestion, mitigate parking issues, and sustain the area's natural resources. Traffic patterns, parking lots, and trailhead locations may change because of this plan; check with park staff at entrance stations or the visitor center for the most current information. Also, learn more about bison at the park's new Bison Education Center, located on the Wildlife Loop near the buffalo corrals.

The magnificent granite formations of Custer State Park JOAN F. CARROLL

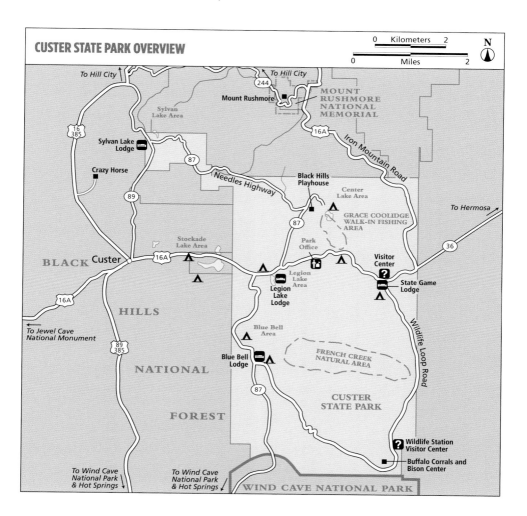

CUSTER STATE PARK OVERVIEW

34 **SUNDAY GULCH TRAIL**

A trail that loops behind Sylvan Lake and offers some of the best overviews of the park's exquisite diversity. The trail is closed in winter.

Start: From the Sylvan Lake Shore Trail, going behind the dam to the Sunday Gulch trailhead
Elevation gain: 5,607 to 6,306 feet
Distance: 4.0-mile lollipop
Difficulty: Strenuous due to steep, slippery ascents and descents
Hiking time: 2 to 3 hours
Seasons: Best early June through fall; closed in winter
Fees and permits: Park entrance fee
Trail contact: Custer State Park, 13329 US Hwy. 16A, Custer, SD 57730; (605) 255-4515; https://gfp.sd.gov/parks/

Dog-friendly: Leashed dogs permitted
Trail surface/conditions: Forested trail, rocks, stream
Land status: Custer State Park
Nearest town(s): Custer
Other trail users: Mountain bikers
Maps: Black Hills National Forest Map; National Geographic/Trails Illustrated Topo Map No. 238
Trailhead amenities: Available throughout the Sylvan Lake area
Maximum grade: 12.1% for 1.1 miles

FINDING THE TRAILHEAD

From the Custer State Park Visitor Center, take US 16A west, then take SD 87 north then west to Sylvan Lake, a total distance of about 19 miles. Park in the day-use parking lot.

Or come in at the Sylvan Lake entrance station via US 16/385 south from Hill City to SD 87 south to Sylvan Lake.

From the city of Custer, take SD 89 north for approximately 6 miles to Sylvan Lake.

Walk the Sylvan Lake Shore Trail west for 0.4 mile to the trailhead sign on the right.
GPS: N43 50.854' / W103 33.978'

THE HIKE

The Sunday Gulch Trail is considered so extraordinary in its spectrum of plants, trees, mosses, and great scenery that it was designated a National Recreation Trail in 1971. The Sunday Gulch trailhead is located behind Sylvan Lake. You will need to hike 0.4 mile on the north side of the lake to reach the trailhead. The length of the Sunday Gulch Trail itself is 3.2 miles, but the total hike will be closer to 4.0 miles when starting and ending at the Sylvan Lake parking lot.

As you hike counterclockwise, the trail immediately descends steeply for 0.25 mile, winding over huge rocks as it drops into the depths of Sunday Gulch. The rocks can be slippery; some stone steps and handrails are provided for the first portion of the hike. Exercise caution.

As you begin the descent, huge granite walls tower on each side of the trail, which parallels the creek as it drops into the ravine. Various rock layers and formations exist here (quartzite, schist, and granite). Tiny waterfalls and rock grottoes surrounded by ponderosa pine, Black Hills spruce, paper birch, and aspen provide photo opportunities.

Plan on wet feet. Old man's beard, a gray-green lichen, hangs from the trees, adding to the mystery of the gulch. Many of the rocks are covered with mosses and lichen.

The trail reaches its lowest point after 1.5 miles of hiking, then begins to ascend. As the trail ascends from the gulch, beautiful panoramas of the granite formations slide into view. You will encounter power lines, and at times the trail parallels the road; still, the beauty of the area is not diminished. The trail is well marked with blue diamonds on trees.

Social trails abound along the Sunday Gulch Trail. Remember to stay on designated trails and follow the trails markings on trees to know you are headed in the right direction.

The descent through Sunday Gulch requires the use of a series of steps and railings

MILES AND DIRECTIONS

0.0 The Sunday Gulch Trail begins behind Sylvan Lake, which requires a 0.4-mile walk to the trailhead from the parking lot.

0.4 Reach the Sunday Gulch trailhead; hike the loop counterclockwise.

1.5 The trail reaches its lowest point near power lines; here the trail begins its ascent.

2.1 The trail begins to parallel SD 87.

3.6 The trail ends at the junction with the Sylvan Lake Shore Trail; going left will take you back the same way you came; heading right will continue the circle around Sylvan Lake.

4.0 Arrive back at the Sylvan Lake parking lot.

View from one of the higher points along the Sunday Gulch Trail

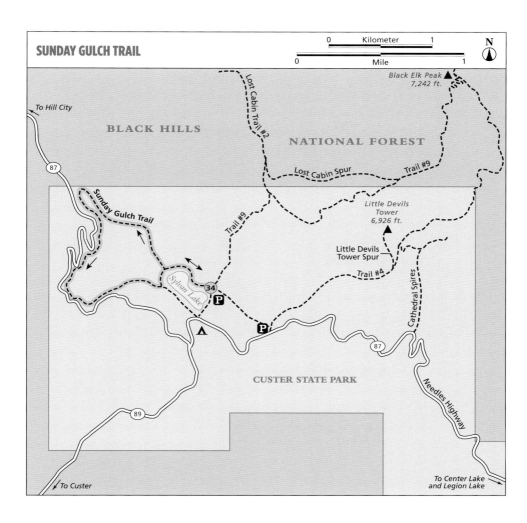

SUNDAY GULCH TRAIL

0   Kilometer   1

0   Mile   1

N

To Hill City

BLACK HILLS

NATIONAL FOREST

Black Elk Peak
7,242 ft.

Lost Cabin Trail #2

Lost Cabin Spur

Trail #9

87

Sunday Gulch Trail

Trail #9

Little Devils
Tower
6,926 ft.

Little Devils
Tower Spur

Sylvan Lake

34

P

Trail #4

Cathedral Spires

P

87

Needles Highway

CUSTER STATE PARK

89

To Custer

To Center Lake
and Legion Lake

35 LOVERS' LEAP TRAIL

A loop trail passing through a ponderosa pine and oak forest, offering great views at the summit. While hiking be on the lookout for bison, deer, coyotes, and bighorn sheep.

Start: At the trailhead behind the schoolhouse and near the outdoor wedding pavilion, across from the Peter Norbeck Outdoor Education Center
Elevation gain: 4,207 to 4,780 feet
Distance: 4.2-mile lollipop
Difficulty: Strenuous at first due to steep incline, then moderate
Hiking time: 2 to 3 hours
Seasons: Best late spring through fall
Fees and permits: Park entrance fee
Trail contact: Custer State Park, 13329 US Hwy. 16A, Custer, SD 57730;

(605) 255-4515; https://gfp.sd.gov/parks/
Dog-friendly: Leashed dogs permitted
Trail surface/conditions: Rocky, forested trail
Land status: Custer State Park
Nearest town(s): Custer, Hermosa
Other trail users: Mountain bikers, horseback riders
Maps: National Geographic/Trails Illustrated Topo Map No. 238
Trailhead amenities: Available at nearby visitor center
Maximum grade: 10.5% for 0.7 mile

FINDING THE TRAILHEAD

The trail begins behind the schoolhouse across from the Peter Norbeck Outdoor Education Center on US 16A, less than 1 mile west of the Custer State Park Visitor Center. GPS: N43 45.840' / W103 22.979'

THE HIKE

According to legend, Lovers' Leap derives its name from a Native American couple who elected to end their lives by plummeting from the lofty outcropping of rocks on a 200-foot ridge. Just why the couple leaped to their deaths is not remembered.

The overlook is reached by following the broad trail from behind the schoolhouse, where it immediately begins a relatively steep climb through bur oak and ponderosa pine forest. You reach the loop after just 0.2 mile; keep left (hiking clockwise) to continue the ascent. You can choose to hike the loop in either direction, but hiking clockwise lets you get the hard part over with first. Also, when hiking clockwise, the Lovers' Leap site is only about 1.0 mile from where the loop begins; once you reach Lovers' Leap, the 3.0 miles that remain are mostly downhill. Alternatively, if you just want to hike to the summit and then retrace your steps back to the trailhead the way you came and not take the loop, the total length of the hike is only 2.5 miles, shaving off about 1.7 miles.

Near the trail's highest point, a sign greets you and provides the following message: "Custer State Park is a place where one can still be an unworried and unregimented individual and wear any old clothes and sit on a log and get their sanity back again." Beyond the trail and sign, you can climb the short distance through the boulders (to your right) and reach the deadly "lovers' leap" point.

The view from the summit (elevation 4,780 feet) is spectacular. Be careful and watch your footing. Across the valley and in the near distance are the charred remains of the

Legion Lake Fire of 2017 and the Galena Fire of 1988. Looking beyond, on clear days, you can see both Black Elk Peak and the Cathedral Spires to the northwest, Mount Coolidge to the southwest (look for the mountain with towers on the top of it), and the plains to the east.

Leaving Lovers' Leap and continuing on the loop, the trail descends the west side of the ridge to Galena Creek. Just before the first stream crossing, the Galena Horse Trail veers off to the left; make sure to keep right. The trail then meanders along the narrow creek bed and makes several stream crossings via recently constructed wooden planks. Poison ivy abounds along the creek bed and the trail, so wear long pants and watch where you place your feet. In addition to ponderosa pine and bur oak, there are also birch trees along this section of the trail.

After the final stream crossing, the trail slightly ascends the ridge again and passes behind the park's employee housing and the Coolidge General Store. Another trail split is reached at mile 3.4; keep right to continue on the main trail. About a half mile later, you will close the loop at the stem, which will return you to the trailhead.

MILES AND DIRECTIONS

0.0 Start at the trailhead behind the schoolhouse across from the Peter Norbeck Outdoor Education Center.

0.2 Join the loop here and keep left (east/southeast), hiking clockwise.

1.25 Sign with quote is reached, climb to the rocky overlook on your right. Watch your footing. Continuing on the loop, the trail begins its descent to Galena Creek.

Inspirational quote near the Lovers' Leap spot

2.0 Begin a series of stream crossings.

3.4 Trail split; keep right (in an easterly direction).

4.0 The trail returns to the stem; turn left (northeast) and follow the trail back to the trailhead parking lot.

4.2 Arrive back at the trailhead.

Galena Creek along the Lovers' Leap Trail

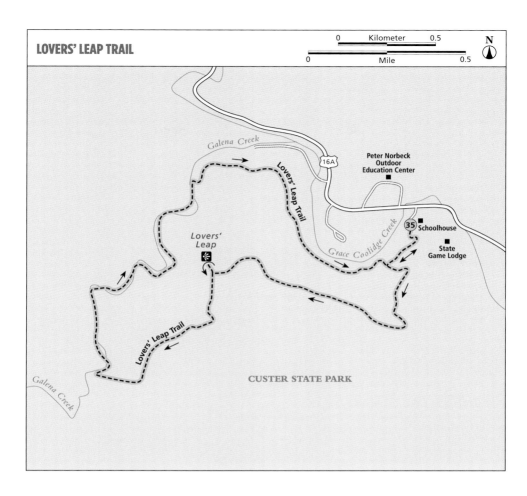

LOVERS' LEAP TRAIL

0 .... Kilometer 0.5

0 .... Mile 0.5

N

Galena Creek

16A

Peter Norbeck
Outdoor
Education Center

Grace Coolidge Creek

Lovers' Leap Trail

Lovers'
Leap

35 Schoolhouse

State
Game Lodge

Lovers' Leap Trail

Galena Creek

CUSTER STATE PARK

36 GRACE COOLIDGE WALK-IN FISHING AREA

A beautiful, fairly flat walk, beginning at either Grace Coolidge Campground or Center Lake, that parallels (with many crossings) Grace Coolidge Creek.

Start: Either across the road from the Grace Coolidge Campground (southern trailhead) or at Center Lake (northern trailhead) near the shower house
Elevation gain: 4,423 to 4,807 feet
Distance: 5.0 miles out and back
Difficulty: Easy
Hiking time: 2 to 3 hours
Seasons: Best late spring through fall
Fees and permits: Park entrance fee; fishing license required if you plan to fish
Trail contact: Custer State Park, 13329 US Hwy. 16A, Custer, SD 57730;

(605) 255-4515; https://gfp.sd.gov/parks/
Dog-friendly: Leashed dogs permitted
Trail surface/conditions: Dirt road
Land status: Custer State Park
Nearest town(s): Custer
Other trail users: Mountain bikers, horseback riders
Maps: National Geographic/Trails Illustrated Topo Map No. 238
Trailhead amenities: None; available at nearby visitor center
Maximum grade: 3% for 2.4 miles

FINDING THE TRAILHEAD

To find the southern trailhead, take US 16A west from the Custer State Park Visitor Center for 2.5 miles. The trailhead is on the right (north side of the road), across the road from the Grace Coolidge Campground. Follow signs to the trailhead parking lot. GPS: N43 46.817' / W103 24.081'

To access the northern trailhead, take US 16A west for 6 miles from the Custer State Park Visitor Center to SD 87. Proceed north on SD 87 for 3 miles to the turnoff for Center Lake and the Black Hills Playhouse, then go 1 mile to Center Lake. The trailhead is located by the shower house near the beach. GPS: N43 48.182' / W103 25.189'

The hike description that follows begins at the southern trailhead.

THE HIKE

The Grace Coolidge Walk-in Fishing Area Trail is an easy and refreshing hike, and the numerous crossings over the narrow, sometimes deep creek add to the fun. Six low-head dams, built by the Civilian Conservation Corps (CCC) in the 1930s, exist along the way, some with deep, dark pools lying beneath granite rock formations. Walking this trail is a fun outing for the entire family. In 1927 President Calvin Coolidge and his wife Grace maintained a summer White House nearby; as a result, many features in the area bear the Coolidge name.

In summer the trail is alive with the vibrant colors of wildflowers and lush green foliage; in fall the bur oak and birch tree leaves add a startling gold that contrasts with the green-black of the ponderosa pines. As in many low, wet areas, poison ivy is abundant along the trail and by the creek.

Closer to Center Lake, the Grace Coolidge Walk-in Fishing Area Trail connects to the Lost Trails system. Signs with trail information and a map of the trail system are located near the shower house at Center Lake. One of the Lost Trails circles around the lake.

MILES AND DIRECTIONS

0.0 Start at the trailhead across the road from the Grace Coolidge Campground (southern trailhead).

2.2 Junction with the Lost Trails system; proceed straight (in a northerly direction) to remain on the Grace Coolidge Trail.

2.5 Arrive at the northern trailhead at Center Lake; turn around and retrace your steps to the southern trailhead.

5.0 Arrive back at the southern trailhead parking lot.

Grace Coolidge Creek

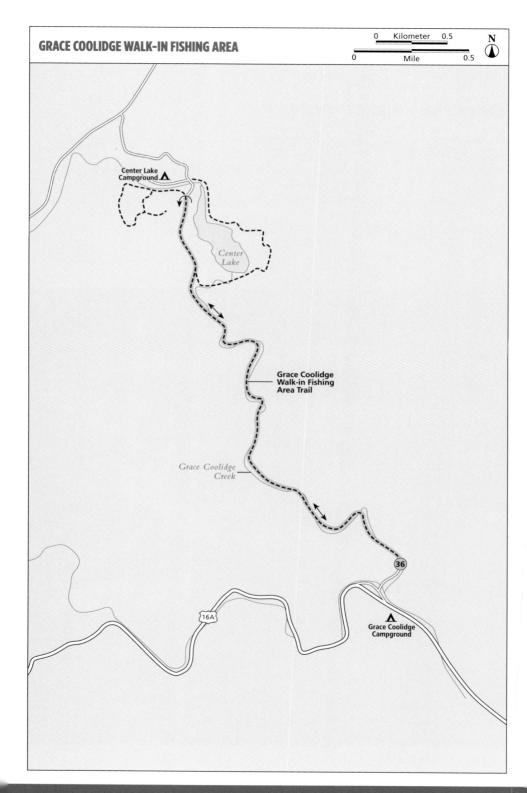

Center Lake Campground

Center Lake

Grace Coolidge Walk-in Fishing Area Trail

Grace Coolidge Creek

36

16A

Grace Coolidge Campground

BLACK ELK RANGE

Black Elk Peak is a significant mountain because it is the highest point in South Dakota and has long been referred to as the highest peak east of the main chain of the Rocky Mountains.

Black Elk Peak's features enchant hikers who follow trails to the peak's 7,242-foot summit (although Black Elk Peak has been surveyed at 7,244 feet, official US Forest Service maps still say 7,242). From the historic lookout tower atop the summit, hikers have distant panoramic views of South Dakota, Nebraska, Wyoming, and Montana, as well as close-up vantage points of the granite formations and cliffs of the Black Elk Wilderness.

The Civilian Conservation Corps (CCC) constructed the stone fire tower in 1938 and 1939. The CCC also constructed stone steps leading to the tower, steps that hikers still ascend today. The tower was used for detecting fires until 1967, when more modern techniques of spotting fires took over. In 1982 the structure was added to the National Register of Historic Places.

The peak's name officially changed to Black Elk Peak (previously Harney Peak) on August 11, 2016, in honor of Black Elk, an Oglala Lakota holy man. The Black Elk Range is a part of the central crystalline core of the Black Hills region and consists mostly of Harney Peak Granite, a type of pegmatitic rock that intruded about 1.7 billion years ago. (A quick note on geologic/geographic names: Harney Peak Granite is still the geologic name for these granite rock formations even though Harney Peak's geographic name changed to Black Elk Peak in 2016.)

Note: The Black Elk Wilderness is managed by the US Forest Service. As of November 2021, mandatory registration for those entering the Black Elk Wilderness to recreate is no longer required. Bikes are not allowed on most trails in this area. Drones are not permitted within the Black Elk Wilderness.

View of the Black Elk Range

The Black Elk Wilderness is a special place; make sure to pack out everything you bring in

SAFETY IN THE BLACK ELK WILDERNESS

In January 2023, I sat down with Custer County Search and Rescue (CCSAR) director Samuel Smolnisky to learn more about safety recommendations for hiking in the Black Elk Wilderness and surrounding areas.

CCSAR was formed in 1973 and is a volunteer organization that provides search, rescue, and other emergency services to people in and around Custer County.

In 2022 the organization responded to nearly one hundred emergency calls, with 32.6 percent of those calls involving a medical rescue and 21.1 percent involving searches for missing hikers. The overwhelming majority of the calls were for emergencies along Trail #9 to Black Elk Peak, the Little Devils Tower Trail, and the Sunday Gulch Trail during the months of June, July, and August.

In addition to the following safety tips, refer to Appendix A: Suggested Equipment in the back of the book for advice on what to bring along on your hike.

- Prepare for the hike in advance.
  - Plan out the hike before you leave.
  - Study and bring along a map.
  - Leave an itinerary with someone (which trailhead you will be parking at, where you will be hiking, your expected return, etc.).
  - Have a backup plan in case of inclement weather.
- Always bring enough water.
  - CCSAR responds to many calls where hikers have become overheated and dehydrated.
  - Dehydration can lead to other problems, such as exacerbating an underlying medical condition.
- Bring your cell phone or alternative device.
  - Make sure your cell phone is fully charged before departing.
  - Emergency services can triangulate your position and pinpoint your location based on where your cell phone is located.
  - If lost on a trail and there is no medical emergency, CCSAR can talk you through where you are and where to go to arrive back at the trailhead.
  - If it gets dark, your cell phone can be used as a flashlight.
  - Personal locator beacons such as SPOT or Garmin inReach are valuable in an emergency.
- If there is an emergency:
  - Call 911 before calling friends and family (secondhand reports make it difficult to locate hikers in the wilderness).
  - Dispatch will automatically direct your emergency to CCSAR.
  - CCSAR is a free service and does not charge hikers for rescue efforts.

Smolnisky stressed the point that the Black Elk Wilderness does not have many trail markers or wayfinding posts because of its wilderness designation.

Also, pay attention to your surroundings. The majority of CCSAR medical emergencies are for sprained or broken ankles, wrists, and arms; dislocated shoulders; and impact trauma to the head due to distracted hikers tripping and falling down on rocks or other hard surfaces.

Sylvan Lake is located within the boundaries of Custer State Park but borders the Black Elk Wilderness. CCSAR receives calls to Sylvan Lake because families become separated while hiking around the lake. The Sunday Gulch trailhead is located behind Sylvan Lake, and it is very easy to take this trail, which is strenuous, instead of continuing around the lake. Oftentimes children, who enthusiastically hike faster than their parents or guardians, end up at the bottom of Sunday Gulch, creating a tense and worrisome situation for the rest of the family.

37 **SYLVAN LAKE TO BLACK ELK PEAK**

A difficult, heavily used trail to the top of Black Elk Peak with remarkable and varied scenery along the way. The peak is the highest point in South Dakota and has long been referred to as the highest peak east of the main chain of the Rocky Mountains. The trail has a total elevation gain of more than 1,450 feet.

Start: At the Sylvan Lake day-use area in Custer State Park
Elevation gain: 6,112 to 7,242 feet
Distance: 6.8 miles out and back
Difficulty: Strenuous due to steep final ascent
Hiking time: 4 to 6 hours
Seasons: Best late spring through fall
Fees and permits: Park entrance fee (Custer State Park)
Trail contacts: Custer State Park, 13329 US Hwy. 16A, Custer, SD 57730; (605) 255-4515; https://gfp.sd.gov/parks/; and Black Hills National Forest Supervisor's Office, 1019 N. 5th St., Custer, SD 57730; (605) 673-9200; www.fs.usda.gov/bhnf

Dog-friendly: Leashed dogs permitted
Trail surface/conditions: Forested trail
Land status: Custer State Park; Black Hills National Forest (Black Elk Wilderness)
Nearest town(s): Custer, Hill City
Other trail users: Horseback riders
Maps: National Geographic/Trails Illustrated Topo Map No. 238; BHNF Black Elk Wilderness and Norbeck Wildlife Preserve Trail System Map; Black Hills National Forest Map
Trailhead amenities: Available throughout the Sylvan Lake area
Maximum grade: 10.7% for 1.5 miles

FINDING THE TRAILHEAD

From just east of the city of Custer, take SD 89 north for 6 miles to the Sylvan Lake entrance station. Follow signs to Sylvan Lake. The trailhead can be found to the north of the day-use parking lot.

From the Custer State Park Visitor Center, take US 16A west, then SD 87 north and west to Sylvan Lake, a total distance of about 19 miles. Park in the day-use parking lot. GPS: N43 50.796' / W103 33.607'

THE HIKE

Hiking traffic on this trail is very heavy at times, especially during summer. This is the most-used route to Black Elk Peak. If possible, consider using an alternate trailhead to begin your hike to the peak (see Hikes 38 and 40).

Heading northeast from Sylvan Lake, the trail provides an easy-to-moderate ascent for the first mile, then descends gently to the area near Lost Cabin Creek, entering the Black Elk Wilderness. This area has no facilities. Water from the creek should not be consumed unless purified or filtered. During the initial ascent, you will encounter a rocky outcrop with outstanding views of Black Elk Peak and its surroundings.

The trail ascends once more, reaching a ridge that is fairly flat. After 2.8 miles of hiking, the Norbeck Trail #3 joins the trail from the right (south). Trail #3 can be used to connect to Trails #4 (to Little Devils Tower) and #7 (Grizzly Bear Creek). Continue north, following the "#9" blazes on trees. The final ascent is steep with several switchbacks. It is flanked by stands of ponderosa pine and granite formations; in spring and summer wildflowers abound. Close to the summit, the trail is sprinkled with mica.

Stone and mortar steps facilitate the last climb through the rocks. The final ascent to the top, at 7,242 feet, is worth the effort. The views of four different states rolling off and eventually merging with the horizon are inspiring. To the northeast, in the not-so-great distance, looms the back side of Mount Rushmore, while to the south, at a distance of about 1 mile, rugged Little Devils Tower juts out from the forest.

Because of Black Elk Peak's grandeur, be prepared for crowds. Summer thunderstorms are frequent and can produce hail and lightning. At times the sun blazes, so carry plenty of water, especially in summer. The trail has a total elevation gain of more than 1,450 feet, so be prepared.

MILES AND DIRECTIONS

0.0 Start at the Sylvan Lake day-use area. Access Black Elk Peak Trail #9, heading northeast.

0.7 The Lost Cabin Trail #2 enters from the left (north). Stay on #9 to your right (east).

1.7 Enter the Black Elk Wilderness (Black Hills National Forest); you are now leaving the boundaries of Custer State Park.

1.8 The Lost Cabin Spur Trail enters from the left (west); continue on Trail #9.

2.8 Junction with Norbeck Trail #3 from the right (south/southeast) along with a sign for Trails #7 and #4. Remain on Trail #9 to continue your hike to Black Elk Peak.

3.1 Turn left (west) at the sign, "Black Elk Peak and Harney Lookout," with an arrow.

3.4 Arrive at Black Elk Peak. Return to Sylvan Lake via the same route.

6.8 Arrive back at the trailhead.

Sylvan Lake

Harney Fire Tower atop Black Elk Peak

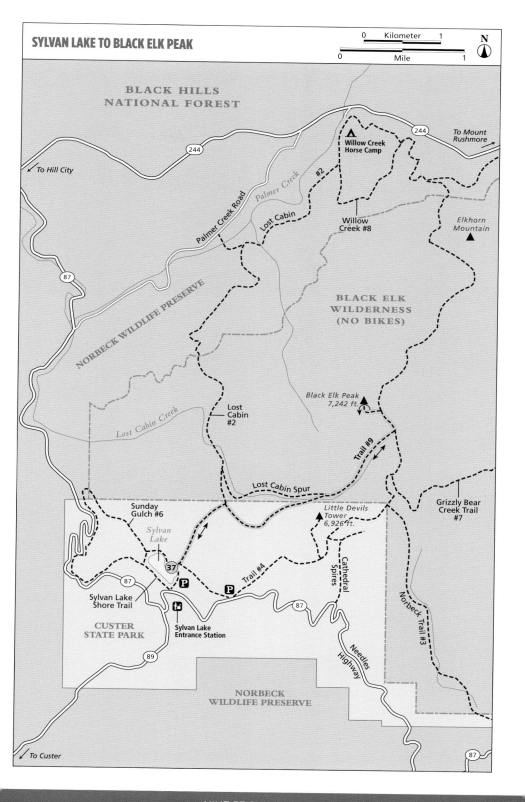

0   Kilometer   1

0   Mile   1

N

BLACK HILLS
NATIONAL FOREST

244

To Hill City →

Palmer Creek Road

Palmer Creek

Lost Cabin

#2

Willow Creek Horse Camp

244

To Mount Rushmore →

Willow
Creek #8

Elkhorn
Mountain

87

NORBECK WILDLIFE PRESERVE

BLACK ELK
WILDERNESS
(NO BIKES)

Lost Cabin Creek

Lost
Cabin
#2

Black Elk Peak
7,242 ft.

Trail #9

Lost Cabin Spur

Grizzly Bear
Creek Trail
#7

Sunday
Gulch #6

Sylvan
Lake

Little Devils
Tower
6,926 ft.

37

Trail #4

Cathedral
Spires

Norbeck Trail #3

87

Sylvan Lake
Shore Trail

P

P

87

CUSTER
STATE PARK

Sylvan Lake
Entrance Station

89

Needles
Highway

NORBECK
WILDLIFE PRESERVE

To Custer →

87

38 LITTLE DEVILS TOWER TRAILHEAD TO BLACK ELK PEAK

A pleasant walk through the woods with the option of linking up with several trails to Black Elk Peak.

Start: At the east end of the Little Devils Tower parking lot, less than a mile east of Sylvan Lake
Elevation gain: 6,267 to 7,242 feet
Distance: 6.6 miles out and back
Difficulty: Strenuous due to steep final ascent
Hiking time: 4 to 6 hours
Seasons: Best late spring through fall
Fees and permits: Park entrance fee
Trail contacts: Custer State Park, 13329 US Hwy. 16A, Custer, SD 57730; (605) 255-4515; https://gfp.sd.gov/parks/; and Black Hills National Forest Supervisor's Office, 1019 N. 5th St., Custer, SD 57730; (605) 673-9200; www.fs.usda.gov/bhnf

Dog-friendly: Leashed dogs permitted
Trail surface/conditions: Forested trail
Land status: Custer State Park; Black Hills National Forest (Black Elk Wilderness)
Nearest town(s): Custer, Hill City
Other trail users: Horseback riders
Maps: National Geographic/Trails Illustrated Topo Map No. 238; BHNF Black Elk Wilderness and Norbeck Wildlife Preserve Trail System Map; Black Hills National Forest Map
Trailhead amenities: Vault toilet
Maximum grade: 13.6% for 0.9 mile

FINDING THE TRAILHEAD

The trail begins at the east end of the Little Devils Tower parking lot, which is located less than a mile east of Sylvan Lake on SD 87 (Needles Highway).

From just east of the city of Custer, take SD 89 north for 6 miles to the Sylvan Lake entrance station. Turn right on SD 87 and proceed to the Little Devils Tower parking lot, on your left (north side of the road).

From the Custer State Park Visitor Center, take US 16A west, then SD 87 north and west to the trailhead on your right, a total distance of about 18 miles. GPS: N43 50.590' / W103 33.152'

THE HIKE

Oftentimes the trail to Black Elk Peak beginning from Sylvan Lake is crowded with nowhere to park at the trailhead. This hike provides an alternative route to Black Elk Peak by starting at the Little Devils Tower trailhead parking lot, which is less than a mile east of Sylvan Lake and affords better parking opportunities. By taking this route, you also will pass by the awe-inspiring Cathedral Spires formations.

The trail, blazed with "#4," begins as an easy, flat hike through the woods, and then ascends for about 1.0 mile to a trail junction. This could be a turnaround point for a short walk. If you wish to continue hiking, stay to the right (in a northeasterly direction) at the junction; the trail to the left is the spur to Little Devils Tower (Hike 39).

Continuing on Trail #4 and ascending through stands of ponderosa, you will connect with Norbeck Trail #3. Take #3 left (north) for about 1.0 mile and connect with the

Black Elk Peak Trail #9, going straight (north), then follow the signs to the top of Black Elk Peak.

MILES AND DIRECTIONS

0.0 Start at the Little Devils Tower trailhead and begin your hike on Trail #4.

1.0 Junction with Little Devils Tower Spur Trail; keep right (northeast) on Trail #4.

1.2 Junction with the Cathedral Spires Trail; stay on Trail #4 to continue on to Black Elk Peak.

1.8 Junction with Norbeck Trail #3. Turn left (north) on Trail #3. You are now entering the Black Elk Wilderness.

2.3 Grizzly Bear Creek Trail #7 comes in from the right (east/southeast). Stay straight (north) on Trail #3.

2.7 Sylvan Lake/Black Elk Peak Trail #9 comes in from the left (southwest). Access Trail #9, going straight ahead (north).

3.0 Turn left (west) and follow signs to the summit of Black Elk Peak.

3.3 You have reached the top of Black Elk Peak. Retrace your steps to the trailhead.

6.6 Arrive back at the trailhead parking lot.

View of the Black Hills from Black Elk Peak

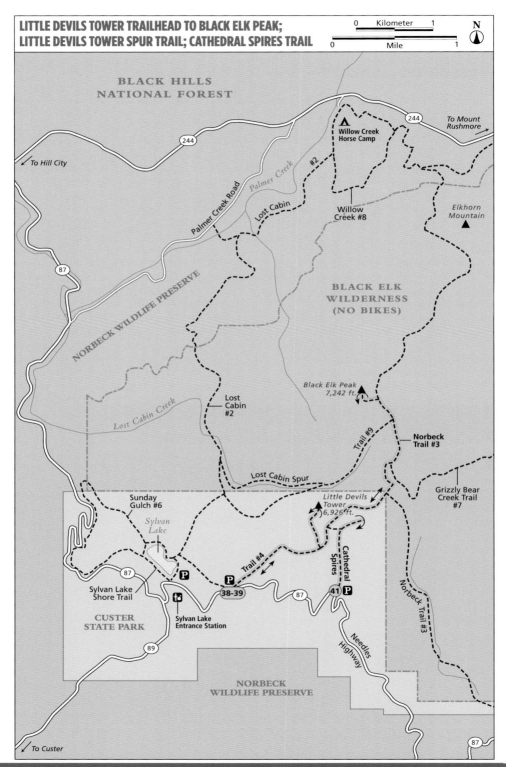

0   Kilometer   1

0   Mile   1

N

BLACK HILLS
NATIONAL FOREST

To Hill City

244

Palmer Creek Road

Palmer Creek

#2

Lost Cabin

Willow Creek Horse Camp

244

To Mount Rushmore

Willow Creek #8

Elkhorn Mountain

87

NORBECK WILDLIFE PRESERVE

BLACK ELK
WILDERNESS
(NO BIKES)

Lost Cabin Creek

Lost Cabin #2

Black Elk Peak
7,242 ft.

Trail #9

Norbeck Trail #3

Lost Cabin Spur

Grizzly Bear Creek Trail #7

Sunday Gulch #6

Sylvan Lake

Little Devils Tower
6,926 ft.

Sylvan Lake Shore Trail

87

P

P

Trail #4

38-39

87

Cathedral Spires

41   P

Norbeck Trail #3

CUSTER
STATE PARK

Sylvan Lake
Entrance Station

Needles Highway

89

NORBECK
WILDLIFE PRESERVE

87

To Custer

87

39 LITTLE DEVILS TOWER SPUR TRAIL

A steep hike winding through forests and ending atop Little Devils Tower among incredible rock formations and views.
See map on page 192.

Start: At the Little Devils Tower parking lot, less than a mile east of Sylvan Lake
Elevation gain: 6,267 to 6,926 feet
Distance: 2.8 miles out and back
Difficulty: Strenuous due to continuous ascent
Hiking time: 2 to 3 hours
Seasons: Best late spring through fall
Fees and permits: Park entrance fee
Trail contact: Custer State Park, 13329 US Hwy 16A, Custer, SD 57730; (605) 255-4515; https://gfp.sd.gov/parks/
Dog-friendly: Leashed dogs permitted

Trail surface/conditions: Forested trail, granite outcroppings (watch your footing)
Land status: Custer State Park
Nearest town(s): Custer, Hill City
Other trail users: Mountain bikers, horseback riders
Maps: National Geographic/Trails Illustrated Topo Map No. 238; BHNF Black Elk Wilderness and Norbeck Wildlife Preserve Trail System Map; Black Hills National Forest Map
Trailhead amenities: Vault toilet
Maximum grade: 8.9% for 1.4 miles

FINDING THE TRAILHEAD

The trail begins at the east end of the Little Devils Tower parking lot, which is less than a mile east of Sylvan Lake on SD 87 (Needles Highway).

From just east of the city of Custer, take SD 89 north for 6 miles to the Sylvan Lake entrance station. Turn right on SD 87 and proceed to the Little Devils Tower parking lot, on your left (north side of the road).

From the Custer State Park Visitor Center, take US 16A west, then SD 87 north and west to the trailhead on your right, a total distance of about 18 miles. GPS: N43 50.590' / W103 33.152'

THE HIKE

Follow Trail #4/Little Devils Tower Trail northeast for about 1.0 mile through stands of quaking aspen and Black Hills spruce. At the first trail junction, take the spur trail to the left (north) to go on to Little Devils Tower (the trail to the right stays on Trail #4 and leads ultimately to Black Elk Peak).

The spur trail begins almost immediately with a fairly steep ascent through ponderosa pine, low-growing juniper, and rocks that look like pancakes turned on edge and stuck in the ground. At mile 1.2, the trail makes a sharp left turn through what appears to be a cave. But this cave has no roof; the walls almost touch at the top, but not quite.

The summit is reached after a very steep hike on granite surfaces (which can sometimes be slippery). Follow the blue diamonds, blue spray paint markings, and rock cairns and ascend to the top of Little Devils Tower. Remember to watch your footing while on top of this massive granite peak. Black Elk Peak is directly across the narrow valley to the north, and you can also see the Cathedral Spires to the southeast. To the northeast is the back side of Mount Rushmore, to the west is the Limestone Plateau, and to the south you can view the rolling Black Hills as they descend to the prairie. In summer the trail is flanked by wildflowers such as buttercups and shooting stars.

After a well-earned rest, hike back down to the Little Devils Tower trailhead. Remember that hiking off-trail in an unmarked area is not recommended or encouraged.

Option: From the west end of the Little Devils Tower parking lot, you may take a short 0.5-mile, marked trail west that leads to Sylvan Lake.

MILES AND DIRECTIONS

0.0 Start at the Little Devils Tower trailhead and begin hiking northeast on Trail #4.

1.0 Take the spur trail to the left (north) to the summit of Little Devils Tower.

1.2 Sharp left turn.

1.4 Arrive at the top of Little Devils Tower. Carefully retrace your steps to the trailhead.

2.8 Arrive back at the trailhead parking lot.

View of the Black Elk Range from atop Little Devils Tower

View of Little Devils Tower in winter

40 LOST CABIN-BLACK ELK PEAK LOOP

A vigorous loop hike through a variety of lofty terrain so beautiful that one of the trails (Lost Cabin) has been designated a National Recreation Trail.

Start: At the Willow Creek Horse Camp trailhead
Elevation gain: 5,016 to 7,242 feet
Distance: 13.3-mile loop
Difficulty: Strenuous
Hiking time: Plan on nearly a full day
Seasons: Best late spring through fall
Fees and permits: No fees or permits required
Trail contact: Black Hills National Forest Supervisor's Office, 1019 N. 5th St., Custer, SD 57730; (605) 673-9200; www.fs.usda.gov/bhnf.
Dogfriendly: Leashed dogs permitted

Trail surface/conditions: Forested trail
Land status: Black Hills National Forest (Norbeck Wildlife Preserve; Black Elk Wilderness)
Nearest town(s): Hill City, Keystone
Other trail users: Horseback riders
Maps: National Geographic/Trails Illustrated Topo Map No. 238; BHNF Black Elk Wilderness and Norbeck Wildlife Preserve Trail System Map; Black Hills National Forest Map
Trailhead amenities: Vault toilets, picnic tables
Maximum grade: 10.9% for 2.0 miles

FINDING THE TRAILHEAD

The trailhead is located at Willow Creek Horse Camp on SD 244, about 3 miles east of the turnoff onto SD 244 from US 16/385.

From the east, Willow Creek Horse Camp is about 4 miles west of Mount Rushmore National Memorial on SD 244 (opposite Palmer Gulch KOA). Park in the grassy parking lot before the campground. Walk into the campground and take the first gravel road to the left. The trail begins past campsites 1–3 at the end of the road. GPS: N43 53.630' / W103 32.163'

THE HIKE

Part of the Black Elk Peak Trail System, this hike may be one of the most picturesque in the wilderness. It is somewhat less strenuous if followed in the direction suggested here, but those desiring a more strenuous hike can reverse the loop. Plan to spend most of a day on this hike; you will want to stop often to absorb the views.

As a trail of such immense appeal, Lost Cabin Trail #2 was designated a National Recreation Trail in 1979. The trail is quickly accessed by departing from Willow Creek Horse Camp and following the signs for Trail #2. Do not confuse this trail with Willow Creek Trail #8, which is also located near the horse camp. The Lost Cabin Trail starts past campsites 1–3 within the Willow Creek Horse Camp (make sure to carefully read "Finding the Trailhead").

The trail immediately ascends through numerous granite outcroppings and stands of ponderosa pine and birch to a saddle. At the saddle the trail begins a series of gentle ups and downs, though the general grade is up. About 1.3 miles from the trailhead, you will cross Nelson Creek. About 0.1 mile later you will encounter a trail junction. The trail to the right (west), leads to the Palmer Creek trailhead. Remain on Lost Cabin Trail #2.

Follow Trail #2 south and ascend to a wide saddle. In July the sides of the trail are sprinkled with a variety of wildflowers. Look for fireweed, Indian paintbrush, harebell, and shooting star. Juniper berries weigh heavy on the low-growing bushes.

The trail levels for a short distance then climbs moderately. At this point the elevation is more than 6,000 feet. After entering the Black Elk Wilderness, the trail undulates mildly, soon crossing a small stream. In summer bunchberry dogwood blossoms by the stream, and the smell of wild mint is strong. Spire and needle formations surround the trail. The Lost Cabin Spur is reached after hiking a total of 4.7 miles; keep to the left and head in a southeast/easterly direction.

The Lost Cabin Spur Trail continues for another 1.3 miles to where it ends as it joins with Black Elk Peak Trail #9. Stay left (east/northeast) on Trail #9, then make a sharp left (north/northwest), climbing 1.4 miles until you reach the Black Elk Peak spur trail on the left (west). Follow the signs and ascend the short, steep trail to the summit of Black Elk Peak.

Descending from Black Elk Peak, resume hiking along Trail #9 by turning left and heading north. The initial descent is steep. For the next mile the trail makes no fewer than thirty switchbacks as it plummets 500 feet. The trail then levels to a saddle offering superb views of Black Elk Peak, the back side of Mount Rushmore, and surrounding spire formations. Here, facing east, one can clearly see the Hogback Ridge (Lakota Formation) and the Red Valley (Spearfish Formation), which engulf the granite formations of the central area of the Black Hills. In the more distant east, the Badlands suggest a great mystery as they blend with the horizon.

For the next 2.0 miles, the trail descends and winds through ponderosa pine, eroded pinnacles and spires, and the boulder fields of Elkhorn Mountain. At mile 12.3, the trail connects with the Willow Creek Trail #8; take this trail to the right (north/northwest) and loop back to your vehicle at the grassy parking area near the Willow Creek Horse Camp.

MILES AND DIRECTIONS

0.0 Start at the Willow Creek Horse Camp trailhead. Head south, following signs for the Lost Cabin Trail #2.

1.3 Cross Nelson Creek.

1.4 The trail to Palmer Creek trailhead comes in from the right (west). Remain on Lost Cabin Trail #2.

4.7 Take the Lost Cabin Spur to the left (southeast/east).

6.0 The trail intersects with Black Elk Peak Trail #9. Turn left here (east/northeast), staying on Trail #9.

7.4 Follow signs to Black Elk Peak.

7.7 Arrive at the top of Black Elk Peak.

8.0 Descending from Black Elk Peak, turn left (north) on Trail #9 toward Willow Creek Horse Camp.

11.2 Willow Creek–Rushmore Trail #5 goes right (east). Continue left (in a northwesterly direction) on Trail #9 toward Willow Creek Horse Camp.

12.3 Turn right (north/northwest) on Willow Creek Trail #8 and loop back to the campground.

13.3 Arrive back at the trailhead.

View of Black Elk Peak from Trail #9 North

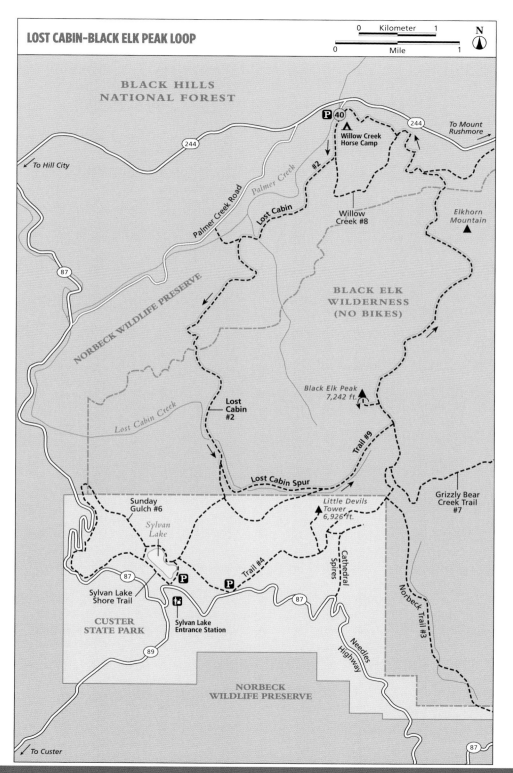

LOST CABIN-BLACK ELK PEAK LOOP

0 Kilometer 1

0 Mile 1

N

BLACK HILLS
NATIONAL FOREST

← To Hill City

244

To Mount
Rushmore →

244

P 40

Willow Creek
Horse Camp

Palmer Creek Road

Palmer Creek

Lost Cabin

#2

Willow
Creek #8

Elkhorn
Mountain

87

NORBECK WILDLIFE PRESERVE

BLACK ELK
WILDERNESS
(NO BIKES)

Lost Cabin Creek

Lost
Cabin
#2

Black Elk Peak
7,242 ft.

Trail #9

Lost Cabin Spur

Grizzly Bear
Creek Trail
#7

Sunday
Gulch #6

Sylvan
Lake

Little Devils
Tower
6,926 ft.

P

P

Trail #4

Cathedral
Spires

Norbeck Trail #3

87

Sylvan Lake
Shore Trail

87

Sylvan Lake
Entrance Station

CUSTER
STATE PARK

89

Needles
Highway

NORBECK
WILDLIFE PRESERVE

← To Custer

87

41 CATHEDRAL SPIRES TRAIL

This strenuous trail is a great natural history trek, offering wonderful views of the spires.
See map on page 192.

Start: At the Cathedral Spires parking lot along the Needles Highway
Elevation gain: 6,212 to 6,670 feet
Distance: 1.8 miles out and back
Difficulty: Strenuous due to continuous steep ascent to the spires
Hiking time: 1 to 2 hours
Seasons: Best late spring through fall
Fees and permits: Park entrance fee
Trail contact: Custer State Park, 13329 US Hwy. 16A, Custer, SD 57730; (605) 255-4515; https://gfp.sd.gov/parks/
Dog-friendly: Leashed dogs permitted

Trail surface/conditions: Rocky dirt path
Land status: Custer State Park
Nearest town(s): Custer
Other trail users: Horseback riders, mountain bikers
Maps: National Geographic/Trails Illustrated Topo Map No. 238; BHNF Black Elk Wilderness and Norbeck Wildlife Preserve Trail System Map; Black Hills National Forest Map
Trailhead amenities: None
Maximum grade: 13.4% for 0.7 mile

FINDING THE TRAILHEAD

The trail is accessed from the Cathedral Spires parking lot, 2 miles east of Sylvan Lake on SD 87 (Needles Highway). You can also access it from the Custer State Park Visitor Center by taking US 16A west for 6 miles to SD 87, then going north for 11 miles. GPS: N43 50.503' / W103 32.117'

THE HIKE

The Cathedral Spires Trail is a strenuous hike that begins at the north end of the parking area. At first the trail is flat, but after crossing a creek it quickly begins its ascent and, with few exceptions, never stops.

The total elevation gain on the trail is about 500 feet. Game trails as well as social trails created by rock climbers lace the area, and because they can at times be confused with the main trail, pay close attention to the progression of blue diamonds marked on trees. If you lose sight of them, simply stay between the confines of the narrow valley walls until you link once again with the main trail.

Once the trail climbs through a narrow "U" of rock bluffs, it widens and becomes much more distinct. When the saddle is reached, a connector trail to Trail #4 (Little Devils Tower) veers off to the left (west); stay on the main Cathedral Spires Trail by turning right (east). The trail dead-ends (look for the sign on a tree) on the north side of the spires at a lookout. Backtrack downhill to the trailhead.

MILES AND DIRECTIONS

0.0   Start at the trailhead on the north side of the Cathedral Spires parking area.

0.9   Reach the "end of the trail" sign. Retrace your steps to the trailhead.

1.8   Arrive back at the trailhead.

The Cathedral Spires

42 IRON MOUNTAIN LOOP

A loop hike taking hikers from mountaintop to forest floor while hiking over streams, into small valleys flanked by rock formations, and through parklike settings cut by beaver dams.

Start: At the Iron Mountain Picnic Area on Iron Mountain Road
Elevation gain: 4,862 to 5,329 feet
Distance: 5.9-mile lollipop
Difficulty: Easy to moderate
Hiking time: 2 to 4 hours
Seasons: Best late spring through fall
Fees and permits: No fees or permits required
Trail contact: Black Hills National Forest Supervisor's Office, 1019 N. 5th St., Custer, SD 57730; (605) 673-9200; www.fs.usda.gov/bhnf
Dog-friendly: Leashed dogs permitted

Trail surface/conditions: Forested trail, dirt road
Land status: Black Hills National Forest (Norbeck Wildlife Preserve, Black Elk Wilderness)
Nearest town(s): Keystone
Other trail users: Horseback riders
Maps: National Geographic/Trails Illustrated Topo Map No. 238; Black Hills National Forest Map; BHNF Black Elk Wilderness and Norbeck Wildlife Preserve Trail System Map
Trailhead amenities: Vault toilets, picnic tables
Maximum grade: 9.2% for 0.3 mile

FINDING THE TRAILHEAD

From the Custer State Park Visitor Center, take US 16A east for about 2 miles. Take a left (north) onto Iron Mountain Road (still US 16A), toward Mount Rushmore, and drive for 12.9 miles to the Iron Mountain Picnic Area on the left (west side of the road). The trail begins at the west end of the parking area for the picnic area.

From Keystone, take US 16A (Iron Mountain Road) south for about 4 miles to the trailhead. GPS: N43 51.262' / W103 26.261'

THE HIKE

The Iron Mountain Loop is a day trip that provides hikers with great vistas and glimpses of the many facets of the Black Hills. This trail is almost entirely in the wilderness, and bikes are not allowed; signs are posted to that effect. From the parking lot, follow the asphalt path past the toilets to access the trailhead.

The trail begins as a wide dirt trail blazed "#89B." It heads west and, at 0.3 mile, joins the Iron Mountain Trail #16, which goes left (south) to begin the loop portion of the hike. The trail is well marked with "#16" blazed on trees.

At mile 1.7 the trail meets an improved gravel road (FR 345). Go right (west/southwest) on the road. Follow the road for about 1.0 mile, where six bridges cross Iron Creek as it meanders through the mountains. Take the next trail to the right (northwest), where the trail sign indicates Grizzly Bear Creek Trail #7. Along this path, you will see inspiring granite formations. In the fall the yellow and rust-colored leaves intermingle with the dark green of the ponderosa pine, lending even more drama to the igneous rock.

After another 0.8 mile the trail takes a hard right (the trail sign indicates Centennial Trail #89) and heads north/northeast for 0.5 mile, where you will encounter yet another junction. Follow the trail signs for 1.8 miles to the right (northeast) on #89B, completing the loop and heading back to the Iron Mountain Picnic Area.

MILES AND DIRECTIONS

0.0 Start at the Iron Mountain Picnic Area trailhead. Take the asphalt path past the toilets to access the trail, blazed "#89B."

0.3 Turn left (south) at the junction with Iron Mountain Trail #16.

1.7 Turn right (west/southwest) on FR 345.

2.8 Turn right (northwest) on Grizzly Bear Creek Trail #7.

3.6 Turn right (north/northeast) at the junction with Centennial Trail #89.

4.1 Trail junction; take the Centennial Bypass (#89B) to the right (northeast).

5.6 Pass by Iron Mountain Trail #16 once again, the beginning of the loop, on the right (south).

5.9 Arrive back at the Iron Mountain Picnic Area trailhead.

Iron Creek

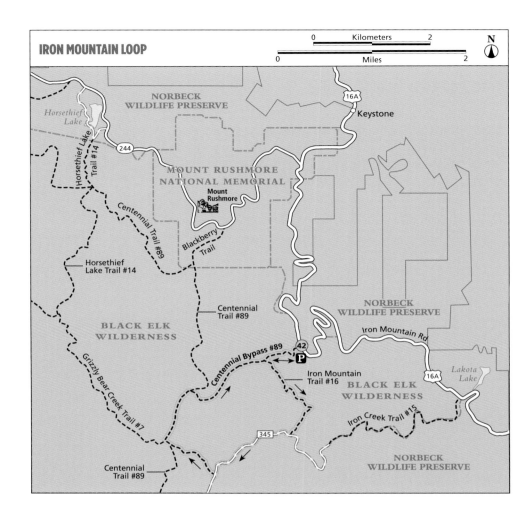

CENTRAL BLACK HILLS— FLUME TRAIL

The Flume Trail is filled with the history of gold mining in the area and is, in addition, a wonderful nature walk. One of many National Recreation Trails in the Black Hills region, the path follows much of an old flume bed. Old parts of the wooden flume can still be seen along this route, as well as other historic artifacts. In the 1880s, the flume transported water from Spring Creek all the way to the Rockerville area, a distance of nearly 20 miles. Hikers cannot help but imagine the gold miners who built the flume with picks, hammers, and shovels. The main section of the Flume Trail is 11 miles one-way (a detailed description of this hike is available in *Hiking the Black Hills Country* by FalconGuides). However, two easy loop trails branch off from the main trail, with Spring Creek Loop B being an easy yet very scenic trail. And a hike up to the top of Boulder Hill is one of the "must-dos" of the central Black Hills.

Tunnel along the main section of the Flume Trail

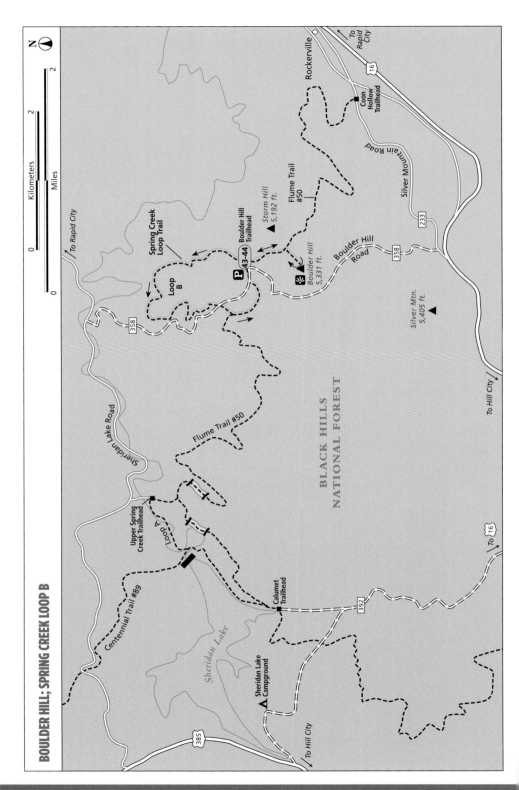

To Rapid City

N

Kilometers

Miles

To Rapid City

Spring Creek
Loop Trail

Boulder Hill
Trailhead

43-44

P

Loop
B

Storm Hill
5,192 ft.

Flume Trail
#50

Boulder Hill
5,331 ft.

Boulder Hill
Road

358

233

Silver Mountain Road

Coon
Hollow
Trailhead

Rockerville

16

To Rapid
City

Silver Mtn.
5,405 ft.

BLACK HILLS
NATIONAL FOREST

358

To Hill City

Sheridan
Lake Road

Flume Trail #50

Flume Trail #50

Upper Spring
Creek Trailhead

Loop A

Centennial Trail #89

Calumet
Trailhead

392

To 16

Sheridan Lake

Sheridan Lake
Campground

385

To Hill City

43 **BOULDER HILL**

A short but steep ascent to the top of a high, rocky outcropping in the central Black Hills, offering dramatic views.

Start: At the Boulder Hill trailhead parking lot on FR 358 (Boulder Hill Road)
Elevation gain: 4,720 to 5,331 feet
Distance: 3.2 miles out and back
Difficulty: Strenuous due to steep ascent over a short distance
Hiking time: 1 to 2 hours
Seasons: Best late spring through fall
Fees and permits: No fees or permits required
Trail contact: Mystic Ranger District, 8221 Mount Rushmore Rd., Rapid City, SD 57702; (605) 343-1567; www.fs.usda.gov/bhnf

Dog-friendly: Leashed dogs permitted
Trail surface/conditions: Forested trail, dirt road, granite
Land status: Black Hills National Forest
Nearest town(s): Rapid City, Hill City
Other trail users: Hikers only
Maps: Black Hills National Forest Map; BHNF Flume Trail Map No. 50; National Geographic/Trails Illustrated Map No. 751
Trailhead amenities: None
Maximum grade: 18.9% for 0.5 mile

FINDING THE TRAILHEAD

From Hill City, take US 16 east for 12 miles and turn left on CR 233 (Silver Mountain Road). After only 0.1 mile, turn left onto FR 358 (Boulder Hill Road). Follow this dirt road for 2.3 miles to the trailhead parking lot. The trail leading to Boulder Hill is on the southeast side of the parking lot. Look for a small, narrow, forested path with a sign that reads "To Boulder Hill." GPS: N43 58.134' / W103 23.922'

THE HIKE

Boulder Hill is one of the special features found along the Flume Trail #50. Located just south of the Spring Creek Loop B Trail (Hike 44) and the Boulder Hill trailhead, this short, steep spur hike up to the 5,331-foot summit is well worth the effort.

A marker adjacent to the Spring Creek Loop Trail points the way around the base of Boulder Hill to the east side, where the narrow trail intersects old logging roads twice, and then ascends quite steeply for several hundred feet through the craggy rocks to the summit. Be on the lookout for an occasional person riding an ATV when the trail meets up with more distinct dirt roads. Because forest roads surround Boulder Hill, be sure to look for trail markings (silver diamonds with the #50) and refer to the Miles and Directions below.

From the peak, the 360-degree vista includes the Badlands and rolling prairies to the east, and the Needles formations and Black Elk Peak to the southwest.

MILES AND DIRECTIONS

0.0 Start at the Boulder Hill trailhead; the trail leading to the hill is on the southeast side of the parking lot.

0.7 Turn right off the main Flume Trail and follow signs to Boulder Hill.

0.9 Turn right at the Boulder Hill junction; the trail narrows.

1.3 The trail winds right, then left on an old road, then turns right again on a narrow, rocky path.

1.6 Arrive at the summit. Carefully retrace your steps.

3.2 Arrive back at the trailhead parking lot.

View from the top of Boulder Hill

44 **SPRING CREEK LOOP B**

A flat loop trail through woods on a ridge above Spring Creek that can be included as an addition to the Flume Trail or simply hiked on its own.

See map on page 206.

Start: At the Boulder Hill trailhead parking lot on FR 358 (Boulder Hill Road)
Elevation gain: 4,557 to 4,720 feet
Distance: 3.8-mile loop
Difficulty: Easy
Hiking time: 1 to 2 hours
Seasons: Best late spring through fall
Fees and permits: No fees or permits required
Trail contact: Mystic Ranger District, 8221 Mount Rushmore Rd., Rapid City, SD 57702; (605) 343-1567; www.fs.usda.gov/bhnf

Dog-friendly: Leashed dogs permitted
Trail surface/conditions: Forested trail
Land status: Black Hills National Forest
Nearest town(s): Rapid City, Hill City
Other trail users: Hikers only
Maps: Black Hills National Forest Map; BHNF Flume Trail Map No. 50; National Geographic/Trails Illustrated Topo Map No. 751
Trailhead amenities: None
Maximum grade: Negligible

FINDING THE TRAILHEAD

The Spring Creek Loop Trail is accessed from the Boulder Hill trailhead. From Hill City, take US 16 east for 12 miles and turn left on CR 233 (Silver Mountain Road). After only 0.1 mile, turn left onto FR 358 (Boulder Hill Road). Follow this dirt road for 2.3 miles to the trailhead parking lot. If you are hiking counterclockwise, the Spring Creek Loop B starts on the east side of the parking lot. GPS: N43 58.134' / W103 23.922'

THE HIKE

Part of the Flume National Recreation Trail, the Spring Creek Loop Trail is marked by silver diamonds with the number "50." The path is signed for foot travel only.

From the trailhead parking lot, hike counterclockwise, following the silver diamonds for Spring Creek Loop B to the north. Do not confuse the Spring Creek Loop Trail with the portion of the Flume Trail that leads to Boulder Hill (these two trails begin directly next to each other). A comfortable, wide forest path, the Spring Creek Loop Trail meanders along a cliff edge and through stands of ponderosa pine.

While hiking along the trail, be on the lookout for the rock and wood remnants of the old flume. After about 1.7 miles, the trail turns south. Continue walking south, following signs that read "Foot Travel Only," and you will soon cross FR 358. While on this section of the trail, you will enjoy wonderful views of Boulder Hill. The trail parallels the road for 0.6 mile, crosses FR 358 once more, then returns to the trailhead.

MILES AND DIRECTIONS

0.0 Start at the Boulder Hill trailhead, along the Flume Trail #50. Head north, in a counterclockwise direction.

3.1 Cross FR 358.

3.7 Cross back over FR 358.

3.8 Arrive back at the Boulder Hill trailhead.

Tall ponderosa pines along the Spring Creek Loop B Trail

WIND CAVE NATIONAL PARK

Wind Cave dates back 320 million years, making it one of the world's oldest caves. Wind Cave has one of the largest displays of boxwork, a fragile lattice formation made of calcite that adorns the cave walls and ceilings. Other rare formations contained in the cave include frostwork, popcorn, and helictite bushes—all whose names are suggestive of their looks.

Pahasapa Limestone provides the basis for these formations that were created by the action of water on soft rock over millions of years. The waters that seeped into the cave did not flow through but sat stagnant, aiding in dissolving Wind Cave's limestone into many passageways.

Wind Cave is a sacred place to Native American nations such as the Cheyenne and the Lakota. One Lakota oral tradition tells an emergence story about the creation inside the cave of the Lakota people, who were eventually instructed by the Creator to emerge to the surface of the Earth.

The first documented people to locate the cave were brothers Jesse and Tom Bingham, who in 1881 heard strange whistling sounds emanating from the ground. The sounds drew them to the hole, which they then showed to others. In the more than 140 years since the cave's discovery, cavers have explored and mapped more than 160 miles of the cave's complex system. For historical perspective, when the National Park Service officially began managing Wind Cave in 1903, fewer than 10 miles of cave were known. By 2001, that number had increased to 100 miles. In 2019 the park celebrated surpassing 150 miles of mapped passageways, and in 2022, more than 160 miles. Additionally, air pressure studies have indicated that only 5 to 10 percent of Wind Cave is currently mapped, leaving the possibility that the cave has hundreds of miles yet to be discovered.

Recognizing the cave's extraordinary features—as well as the extraordinarily beautiful prairie ecosystem above it—Congress sought protection of the Wind Cave complex, and in 1903 Wind Cave became a national park. Visitors may take one of the park-provided, year-round cave tours, led by park personnel.

Though the park is better known for its miles of explored underground passages, visitors can also explore Wind Cave above the ground, in one of the nation's lushest and most pristine prairie grasslands. Here exists an incredible prairie ecosystem and ponderosa pine forest that includes a diverse mix of wildlife roaming freely throughout the park's 33,971 acres. Because motorized vehicles and mountain bikes are confined to the park's roads, hikers who venture onto the park's 30-plus miles of trails are generally rewarded with unparalleled sightings of wildlife. Also be on the lookout for birds such as great horned owls, prairie falcons, cliff swallows, and hawks.

When hiking at Wind Cave, start early, not only to avoid the heat, but also to see the park's wild animals. Bison roam freely within the park's boundaries. With the exceptions of the Elk Mountain and Prairie Vista Nature Trails, you will most likely encounter bison along many of the park's trails. Remember to keep your distance and detour around the large animals to resume your hike. Also be on the lookout for prairie dog holes and rattlesnakes. Check yourself for ticks after hikes. Poison ivy can be found along creeks, and wearing long pants is recommended.

The trails in Wind Cave are all named and numbered. The park charges no entry fee, but there are fees for cave tours.

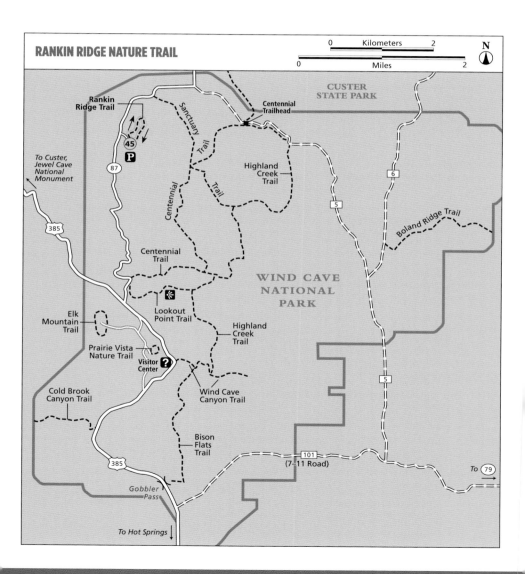

RANKIN RIDGE NATURE TRAIL

0   Kilometers   2

0   Miles   2

N

CUSTER STATE PARK

Rankin Ridge Trail

Sanctuary Trail

Centennial Trailhead

45

P

87

To Custer, Jewel Cave National Monument

Highland Creek Trail

6

5

Centennial Trail

Boland Ridge Trail

385

Centennial Trail

WIND CAVE NATIONAL PARK

Lookout Point Trail

Elk Mountain Trail

Highland Creek Trail

Prairie Vista Nature Trail

Visitor Center

5

Cold Brook Canyon Trail

Wind Cave Canyon Trail

Bison Flats Trail

385

101
(7–11 Road)

To 79

Gobbler Pass

To Hot Springs

Boxwork in Wind Cave National Park Service

45 RANKIN RIDGE NATURE TRAIL

A short, interpretive loop trail that ascends through ponderosa pine forest, providing vistas of Wind Cave National Park and its immense surroundings.

Start: At the Rankin Ridge parking lot off SD 87
Elevation gain: 4,750 to 5,013 feet
Distance: 1.0-mile loop
Difficulty: Easy to moderate
Hiking time: 30 minutes to 1 hour
Seasons: Best spring through fall
Fees and permits: No fees or permits required
Trail contact: Wind Cave National Park, 26611 US Hwy. 385, Hot Springs, SD 57747; (605) 745-4600; www.nps.gov/wica

Dog-friendly: Dogs not allowed
Trail surface/conditions: Forested trail, dirt road
Land status: Wind Cave National Park
Nearest town(s): Hot Springs, Custer
Other trail users: Hikers only
Maps: National Geographic/Trails Illustrated Topo Map No. 238; Wind Cave National Park brochure; Black Hills National Forest Map
Trailhead amenities: None
Maximum grade: 10% for 0.5 mile

FINDING THE TRAILHEAD

Take US 385 north from the park's visitor center to SD 87. Take SD 87 north for about 5 miles to the sign and the road for the fire tower, which is on the right (east side of the road). The Rankin Ridge trailhead is located at the parking lot at the end of this road. GPS: N43 37.369′ / W103 29.150′

THE HIKE

This short trail provides a delightful climb up to the top of Rankin Ridge to see sweeping views. The trail was designated a National Recreation Trail in 1982. The Red Valley (Spearfish Formation) cuts a spectacular swath through the foreground, while the Hogback Ridge (Lakota Formation) suggests a ring engulfing the Black Hills, as described in the Introduction of this book. Buffalo Gap is the "cut" or "break" in the ridgeline to the east. The Badlands, farther to the east, shimmer in the distance when the sun is at your back.

Head out on the trail traveling clockwise in a north/northeasterly direction. Along the way, log benches provide opportunities to rest and further explore the panorama sweeping before you. Bring your binoculars.

Approximately 0.5 mile from the trailhead, you reach the fire tower. A 0.5-mile descent on a dirt road passes through a ponderosa pine forest and returns you to the parking lot.

MILES AND DIRECTIONS

0.0 Start at the trailhead parking lot off SD 87, hiking clockwise.

0.5 Reach the fire tower.

1.0 Arrive back at the trailhead.

View from the top of Rankin Ridge

46 LOOKOUT POINT-CENTENNIAL TRAIL LOOP

A loop hike that offers a chance to explore both prairie and riparian habitats. Bison, deer, pronghorn, and prairie dogs are abundant along the trail.
See map on page 219.

Start: At the Lookout Point/Centennial trailhead off SD 87
Elevation gain: 4,042 to 4,394 feet
Distance: 4.9-mile loop
Difficulty: Moderate
Hiking time: 2 to 4 hours
Seasons: Best spring through fall
Fees and permits: No fees or permits required
Trail contact: Wind Cave National Park, 26611 US Hwy. 385, Hot Springs, SD 57747; (605) 745-4600; www.nps.gov/wica

Dog-friendly: Dogs not allowed
Trail surface/conditions: Dirt path
Land status: Wind Cave National Park
Nearest town(s): Hot Springs
Other trail users: Hikers only
Maps: National Geographic/Trails Illustrated Topo Map No. 238; Wind Cave National Park brochure; Black Hills National Forest Map
Trailhead amenities: Available at nearby visitor center
Maximum grade: 18.9% for 0.1 mile

FINDING THE TRAILHEAD

Take US 385 north from the park's visitor center to SD 87. Take SD 87 north for 0.6 mile to the Lookout Point/Centennial Trail trailhead, which will be on your right (east side of the road). GPS: N43 34.885' / W103 29.028'

THE HIKE

Few trails in the Black Hills offer the opportunity to view both a pristine prairie and a riparian ecosystem.

The hike begins on the south side of the trailhead parking lot, as you will be starting on the Lookout Point Trail, which is marked as Trail #4 on wayfinding posts. The trail immediately descends into a valley and crosses Cold Spring Creek three times. At the final stream crossing, make sure you take a hard right and walk across the wooden footbridge to continue on the trail.

You then ascend up to the prairie, where prairie dog holes flank each side of the trail. After 1.5 miles of hiking, the trail reaches its high point near Lookout Point, elevation 4,403 feet. The trail does not lead directly to Lookout Point, but it is just a short jaunt to your right (south), a grassy knob with scattered ponderosa pine trees.

From here the trail gently descends and cuts through the northern end of Prairie Dog Canyon. Prairie dogs are abundant, and bison encounters should be expected. Keep a safe distance from bison.

At mile 2.2, the trail merges with the Highland Creek Trail (Trail #7) at a junction. Keep left (in a northeasterly direction) to continue on the Lookout Point/Highland

Creek Trails and descend to Beaver Creek, where the landscape quickly changes from prairie to ponderosa pine forest.

Once you reach Beaver Creek, turn left (west) to head back to the trailhead parking lot. From this point the trail crosses the creek numerous times. At mile 3.3, the loop joins the Centennial Trail (Trail #6), which will continue to take you in a westerly direction.

The hike along Beaver Creek offers views of variegated rock bluffs, some a brilliant orange. High caves are cut into the bluffs, and trees that have somehow established a toe-hold stand as sentinels at the entrances to some of these high rock cuts. Along the stream proper, footprints of hikers mingle with those of bison and deer.

As the trail nears its end, waters from Cold Spring Creek merge with those of Beaver Creek, which continues its eastern trend. Near the terminus the trail ascends abruptly and shortly concludes at the Lookout Point/Centennial trailhead.

MILES AND DIRECTIONS

0.0   Start at the Lookout Point/Centennial trailhead on SD 87.

1.5   The trail reaches its highest elevation near Lookout Point, which is on your right (to the south).

2.2   At the Lookout Point/Highland Creek Trail junction, keep left (northeast) on the Lookout Point Trail.

2.8   Reach Beaver Creek; turn left (west).

3.3   At the junction with the Centennial Trail, keep going straight (west) onto the Centennial Trail.

4.9   Arrive back at the Lookout Point/Centennial trailhead.

Lone bison along the Centennial Trail

Sunrise near the Lookout Point/Centennial trailhead

While recently mapping out new sections of Wind Cave, cave explorers discovered an 11,100-year-old pine marten fossil. The fossil still had pieces of hair and skin attached, leading park staff to believe that it was not that old. However, the fossil was sent to Dr. Jim Mead at The Mammoth Site in Hot Springs, where radiocarbon dating estimates have shown the fossil is approximately 11,100 years old. Mead is the director of research at The Mammoth Site and has been studying pine marten fossils found not only in Wind Cave but also in other caves in the area.

"Caves are really nature's museums," said Mead. "Caves are full of secrets of the past and Wind Cave is a classic example."

Mead said that the pine martens who inhabit the Black Hills today were reintroduced to the region a couple of decades ago by wildlife groups and normally do not reside in the southern Hills.

"The pine marten recovered in Wind Cave is the same size and has all the same bone characteristics as today's living pine marten found north, east, and west of the Black Hills," explained Mead. "The fossilized remains had tissue left on the bones allowing for a very accurate age determination, dating to the last Ice Age. The fossil carcass in Wind Cave shows that this small, tree-loving predator related to the weasel used to be in the Black Hills."

Dr. Hazel Barton of the University of Akron collects the fossilized remains of a pine marten that was discovered in Wind Cave. The fossil was sent to the Mammoth Site in Hot Springs, where radiocarbon dating estimates have shown it is around 11,100 years old. NATIONAL PARK SERVICE

LOOKOUT POINT—CENTENNIAL TRAIL LOOP

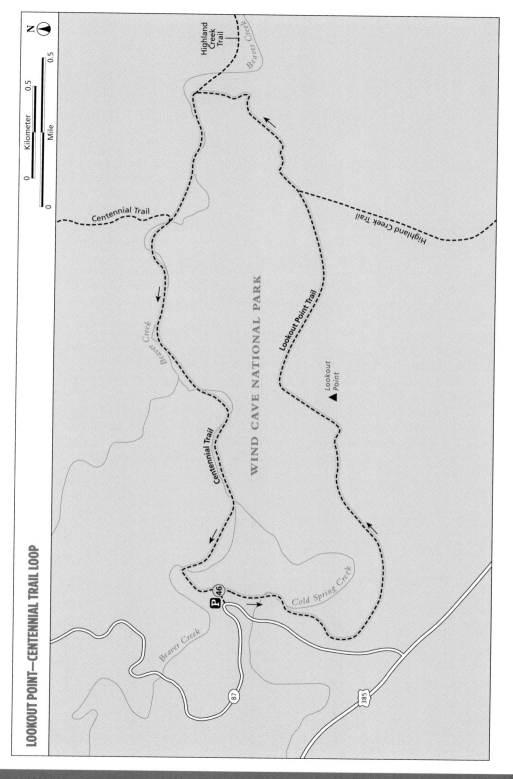

JEWEL CAVE AREA

Currently, Jewel Cave is recognized as the third-longest cave in the world, with more than 200 miles of mapped passageways. The cave began to form approximately 10 to 50 million years ago in the Pahasapa Limestone in the southwestern portion of the Black Hills. Evidence suggests that the cave contains thousands of miles of passageways that have yet to be explored, leading some to believe that it may connect with Wind Cave to the southeast. Unique cave formations such as dogtooth spar, draperies, frostwork, and gypsum flowers can be found inside the cave.

In 1900, two prospectors from the Black Hills heard an interesting sound that they discovered was coming from a small hole in Hell Canyon. The pair decided to use dynamite to enlarge the opening and found themselves inside a cave surrounded by calcite crystals, leading to the name Jewel Cave.

On February 7, 1908, President Theodore Roosevelt proclaimed Jewel Cave a national monument, and the National Park Service began solely operating cave tours in 1939. Today, visitors can choose from a variety of cave tours ranging from easy to strenuous.

Jewel Cave National Monument maintains two hiking trails within its boundary: the Roof Trail and the Canyons Trail. The Hell Canyon Trail, a longer, more demanding hike, is across US 16 from the monument and is managed by the US Forest Service. When hiking these trails, be on the lookout for spring and summer wildflowers, songbirds, and animals such as bighorn sheep, deer, and elk.

There is no fee to hike the surface trails at Jewel Cave National Monument, but there are fees for cave tours.

Cave explorer in Jewel Cave National Park Service

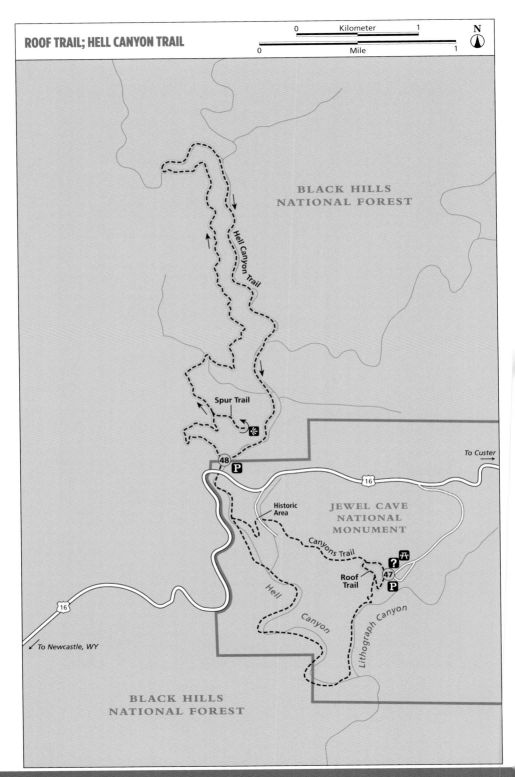

0   Kilometer   1

0   Mile   1

N

BLACK HILLS
NATIONAL FOREST

Hell Canyon Trail

Spur Trail

48

P

To Custer

16

Historic
Area

JEWEL CAVE
NATIONAL
MONUMENT

Canyons Trail

Roof
Trail

47

P

16

Hell

Canyon

Lithograph Canyon

To Newcastle, WY

BLACK HILLS
NATIONAL FOREST

Profile view of George Washington

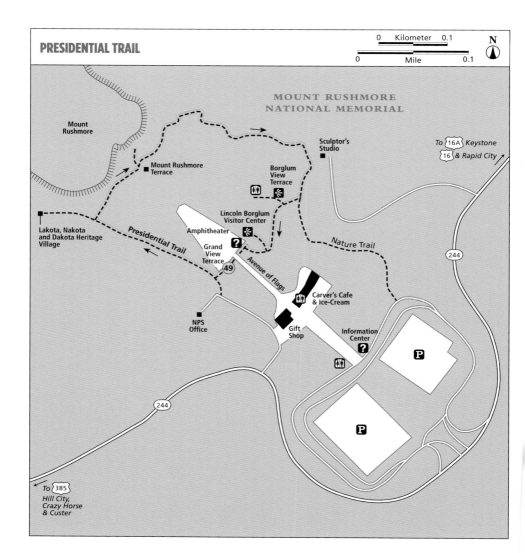

0   Kilometer   0.1

0   Mile   0.1

N

MOUNT RUSHMORE
NATIONAL MEMORIAL

Mount
Rushmore

Sculptor's
Studio

To 16A Keystone
16 & Rapid City

Mount Rushmore
Terrace

Borglum
View
Terrace

Lincoln Borglum
Visitor Center

Lakota, Nakota
and Dakota Heritage
Village

Presidential Trail

Amphitheater

Grand
View
Terrace

49

Avenue of Flags

Nature Trail

244

Carver's Cafe
& Ice-Cream

NPS
Office

Gift
Shop

Information
Center

P

P

244

To 385
Hill City,
Crazy Horse
& Custer

49 PRESIDENTIAL TRAIL

A short walk that allows visitors to view Mount Rushmore from different perspectives.

Start: On the southwest side of the Grand View Terrace past the Avenue of Flags
Elevation gain: 5,234 to 5,364 feet
Distance: 0.6-mile loop
Difficulty: Moderate
Hiking time: 30 minutes to 1 hour
Seasons: Best spring through fall
Fees and permits: Parking fee
Trail contact: Mount Rushmore National Memorial, 13000 Hwy. 244, Bldg. 31, Ste. 1, Keystone, SD 57751; (605) 574-2523; www.nps.gov/moru/

Dogfriendly: Dogs not allowed
Trail surface/conditions: Paved walkway, boardwalk
Land status: Mount Rushmore National Memorial
Nearest town(s): Keystone
Other trail users: Hikers only
Maps: Mount Rushmore National Memorial brochure
Trailhead amenities: Available throughout the memorial
Maximum grade: Negligible

FINDING THE TRAILHEAD

From just west of the town of Keystone, head west on SD 244 and travel 1.5 miles to the Mount Rushmore parking area. The trail begins on the southwest side of the Grand View Terrace past the Avenue of Flags. GPS: N43 52.612' / W103 27.380'

THE HIKE

The Presidential Trail loops around one of the most scenic settings in the Black Hills. The trail can be hiked in either direction, but if wanting to follow the self-guided tour of the memorial, begin on the southwest side of the Grand View Terrace and hike clockwise. Be on the lookout for wildlife as you stop at the different interpretive panels to learn about the memorial. The first 0.1 mile of the trail is accessible, and then the remainder of the loop back to the Grand View Terrace consists of a series of ups and downs on staircases. The trail may be closed in winter.

MILES AND DIRECTIONS

0.0 Start on the southwest side of the Grand View Terrace.

0.1 The trail takes a right turn (northeast).

0.2 Reach the Mount Rushmore Terrace.

0.4 Reach the Sculptor's Studio.

0.6 Arrive back at the Grand View Terrace.

Mount Rushmore

50 HORSETHIEF LAKE TO MOUNT RUSHMORE

An extremely scenic out-and-back hike departing from Horsethief Lake and terminating at Mount Rushmore, with access to other trails, some leading to Black Elk Peak.

Start: At the trailhead parking area on the south side of Horsethief Lake
Elevation gain: 4,871 to 5,494 feet
Distance: 8.0 miles out and back
Difficulty: Moderate
Hiking time: 3 to 4 hours
Seasons: Best late spring through fall
Fees and permits: No fees or permits required
Trail contact: Black Hills National Forest Supervisor's Office, 1019 N. 5th St., Custer, SD 57730; (605) 673-9200; www.fs.usda.gov/bhnf; and Mount Rushmore National Memorial, 13000 Hwy. 244, Bldg. 31, Ste. 1, Keystone, SD 57751; (605) 574-2523; www.nps.gov/moru/

Dog-friendly: Leashed dogs permitted on trail; dogs not allowed inside Mount Rushmore itself
Trail surface/conditions: Forested trail
Land status: Black Hills National Forest (Black Elk Wilderness); Mount Rushmore National Memorial
Nearest town(s): Keystone
Other trail users: Horseback riders
Maps: National Geographic/Trails Illustrated Topo Map No. 238; Black Hills National Forest Map; BHNF Black Elk Wilderness and Norbeck Wildlife Preserve Trail System Map
Trailhead amenities: Vault toilets, picnic tables
Maximum grade: 8% for 1.2 miles

FINDING THE TRAILHEAD

The trailhead is located at the southern end of Horsethief Lake off SD 244. From the junction of US 385/16 between Hill City and Custer, take SD 244 east for about 6.5 miles. Turn right at the Horsethief Lake trailhead sign. From Mount Rushmore, proceed west on SD 244 and look for the trailhead sign on the left (south) side of the road. GPS: N43 53.354' / W103 28.940'

THE HIKE

In the 1930s, the Civilian Conservation Corps (CCC) and the South Dakota Corps of Engineers created Horsethief Lake by building a dam along Pine Creek. This scenic lake is a popular stop along the way to or from Mount Rushmore National Memorial. The fishing is excellent; the lake is home to rainbow trout, golden shiner, and yellow perch.

The trailhead is located on the south side of Horsethief Lake near the day-use area; look for the Black Elk Wilderness information panel. The trail begins on the Horsethief Lake Trail #14. This is a peaceful and very picturesque hike, particularly when birch and aspen leaves are turning in autumn. The trail parallels and crosses a stream with several small, beautiful waterfalls. Granite rock formations rise steeply on each side. *Note*: Horses are not allowed on this section of the trail.

After only 0.6 mile, the trail intersects with the Centennial Trail #89. To continue on to Mount Rushmore, turn left (southeast) on the Centennial Trail. If venturing onto other trails, make sure you have a good map, compass, and enough supplies for a longer hike. At this trail junction, Horsethief Lake Trail #14 continues its southerly route and connects to Grizzly Bear Creek Trail #7. The hike on the Centennial Trail to the west links up with the Willow Creek–Rushmore Trail #5 and leads to the Willow Creek Horse Camp.

As you continue the hike on the Centennial Trail to the southeast toward Mount Rushmore, the trail winds up and down through forests and rocks and reaches its highest elevation of 5,494 feet.

After hiking 2.5 miles on the Centennial Trail, you reach the Blackberry Trail. Turn left at this junction and head in a northerly direction. This portion of the trail is within the boundaries of Mount Rushmore National Memorial and was designated a National Recreation Trail in 2018. At the end of the trail, there is a hitching post for horses and a picnic area. Mount Rushmore can be viewed from this spot.

From the end of the trail near the picnic area, hike back on the same trails to return to the Horsethief Lake parking lot, making this out-and-back trail a total of about 8.0 miles.

MILES AND DIRECTIONS

0.0   Start at the trailhead on the south side of Horsethief Lake.

0.6   Keep left (southeast) on Centennial Trail #89.

3.1   Junction with Blackberry Trail; follow signs that lead to Mount Rushmore.

4.0   End of the trail with views of Mount Rushmore. Retrace your steps to the trailhead.

8.0   Arrive back at the trailhead at Horsethief Lake.

A series of small waterfalls parallel the Horsethief Lake Trail #14

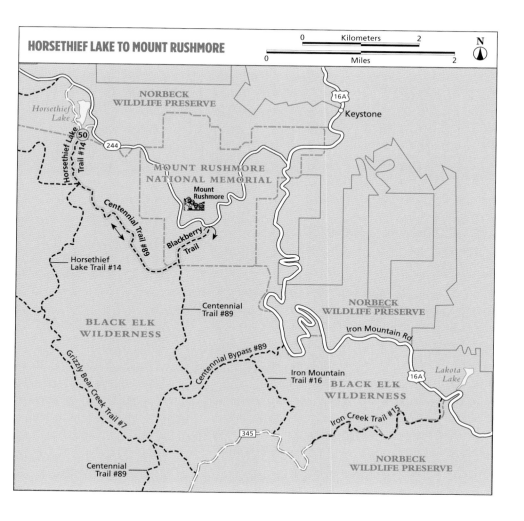

THE LONG TRAILS OF THE BLACK HILLS

CENTENNIAL TRAIL

The land between Wind Cave and Bear Butte is inspiring. Through the combined efforts of different public land agencies, the Centennial Trail was created to celebrate the one hundredth anniversary of South Dakota statehood. This north–south trail cuts through the center of the Black Hills, offering the chance to see magnificent views, wildlife, and other points of interest along the way.

The Centennial Trail is more than 120 miles long. Since the trail is so long and traverses through many different public land agencies, it is only natural that portions of the trail may be rerouted and/or changed over time. Since the trail's establishment in 1989, many sections have been rerouted. Outdated maps and other trail resources may lack the most up-to-date trail information. Hikers are encouraged to research the most current trail information before setting out on the trail, and to use multiple resources. These alterations and any future changes will no doubt modify the total length of the trail. Additionally, different GPS units, watches, and other trail measurement devices will have slight variations. The total length of the trail also depends on which trailheads you use, as there are many different spur trails that lead to optional trailheads.

The Centennial Trail can be backpacked in one grand outing or hiked segmentally over weeks, months, or even years. Mountain bikes are permitted in most areas, except for the nationally designated wilderness areas, such as the Black Elk Wilderness in the Black Hills National Forest and in the National Park Service–administered areas of Wind Cave and Mount Rushmore. Mountain bikes are also not permitted on the trail leading to the summit of Bear Butte. For those planning an extended Centennial Trail trek, finding potable water can be a concern. Carrying a water-purification kit, such as a water filter that is capable of filtering out giardia, is recommended.

Backpackers are encouraged to make primitive use of the land, using zero-impact camping methods. Make sure to practice Leave No Trace ethics.

For those preferring to hike segmentally, the Centennial Trail provides more than twenty trailheads, conveniently located for excursions of 4 to 12 miles.

Trail users will be delighted to learn that, with few exceptions, the Centennial Trail is very well marked. The trail can be hiked in either direction, but it is rewarding to begin at Wind Cave National Park and end atop the summit of Bear Butte.

The author hiking on the Centennial Trail ANDREA FOUNTAIN

MICKELSON TRAIL

The second long trail in the Black Hills is the George S. Mickelson Trail, South Dakota's first rails-to-trails project. It traces the historic Burlington Northern Railroad line for more than 100 miles from Deadwood in the north to Edgemont in the south. When the rail line was abandoned in 1983, local residents recognized the recreational potential of the land. Backed by then-governor George S. Mickelson, the trail was named in his honor. The trail was completed in the fall of 1998, and from end to end it offers a panoramic view of the history and the natural splendor of the heart of the Black Hills.

This trail, with fourteen main trailheads along an old rail bed, offers glimpses into the history of the Black Hills. From it you will see old gold mining camps, claim cabins, cliff cuts, hardrock tunnels, over one hundred converted bridges, high trestles, and pristine streams. In many places the old rail bed is remote enough to offer a backcountry experience. To further enhance your enjoyment and add a greater dimension to your trip, interpretive panels are found along the length of the route. The trail is mostly gravel and crushed rock, with some paved areas in towns.

The trail is open to bikers, skiers, horseback riders, and those on foot. No motorized vehicles are allowed, except for a portion between Deadwood and Dumont that allows snowmobile traffic in winter. Bikers must yield to walkers, and all must yield to horses. The trail is closed from dusk to dawn, and camping is prohibited on the trail right-of-way and at the trailheads. Pets must be on leashes. You will find parking, toilets, and self-sale passes at many of the trailheads. Picnic shelters exist along the trail; one such shelter is at the Hill City trailhead, honoring the Burlington Northern rail line. Much of the trail passes through open range, where cattle freely roam. Make sure to leave gates as you found them, open or closed.

The trail is a part of South Dakota's state park system. To help maintain the trail, users age twelve and older are required to pay a small user fee. Those using the trail within the city limits of towns are not charged a fee. Passes are available at stations along the trail and at some state park offices and local businesses. For information, contact the Black Hills Trail Office (George S. Mickelson Trail), 11361 Nevada Gulch Rd., Lead, SD 57754 (605) 584-3896, or the South Dakota Department of Game, Fish and Parks, 523 E. Capitol Ave., Pierre, SD 57501 (605) 223-7660. The state publishes a trail guide with mileages and trailhead locations along with an elevation profile.

Sources vary on the exact length of the Mickelson Trail, and it depends on where you start and which spur trails you take. However, the trail is marked with large mileposts. Trail users should consult multiple resources before heading out on the trail.

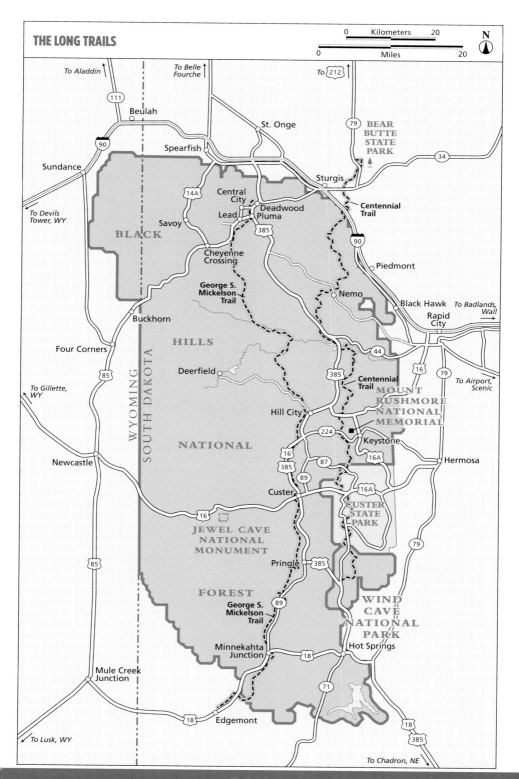

THE LONG TRAILS

0 Kilometers 20
0 Miles 20

N

To Aladdin
To Belle Fourche
To 212

111

Beulah

St. Onge

79 BEAR BUTTE STATE PARK

90

Spearfish

Sundance

34

Sturgis

14A Central City

Centennial Trail

Lead Deadwood Pluma

To Devils Tower, WY

Savoy

BLACK

385

90

Cheyenne Crossing

Piedmont

George S. Mickelson Trail

Nemo

Buckhorn

HILLS

Black Hawk

To Badlands, Wall

Rapid City

Four Corners

85

Deerfield

44

To Gillette, WY

WYOMING SOUTH DAKOTA

385

Centennial Trail

16

79

To Airport, Scenic

MOUNT RUSHMORE NATIONAL MEMORIAL

Hill City

NATIONAL

224

Keystone

Newcastle

16

16A

385

87

Hermosa

89

Custer

16A

JEWEL CAVE NATIONAL MONUMENT

16

CUSTER STATE PARK

FOREST

Pringle

385

79

George S. Mickelson Trail

89

85

WIND CAVE NATIONAL PARK

Minnekahta Junction

18

Hot Springs

Mule Creek Junction

71

18

Edgemont

18

385

To Lusk, WY

To Chadron, NE

GLACIAL MOUNDS TRAIL

A scenic hike in northeastern South Dakota to the top of a ridgeline that was created by glaciers thousands of years ago. The trail is at the east unit of Pickerel Lake Recreation Area.

Start: At the park's campground near the comfort station

Elevation gain: 1,858 to 1,926 feet

Distance: 0.5-mile one-way; the trail begins on the northeast side of the campground and ends on the southern side (walking through the campground back to the trailhead adds an additional 0.2 mile)

Difficulty: Easy

Hiking time: 30 minutes

Seasons: Best spring through fall

Fees and permits: Park entrance fee

Trail contact: Pickerel Lake Recreation Area, 12980 446th Ave., Grenville, SD 57239; (605) 486-4753; https://gfp.sd.gov/parks/

Dog-friendly: Dogs must be on leash or under immediate control

Trail surface/conditions: Mowed grass

Land status: East Pickerel Lake State Recreation Area

Nearest town(s): Grenville, Waubay

Other trail users: Mountain bikers

Maps: State park map

Trailhead amenities: Available throughout park

Maximum grade: 5.1% for 0.25 mile

Glacial Mounds Trail

PHEASANT RUN TRAIL

A pleasant loop hike around the southern shore of Lake Louise, with the opportunity to see different types of waterfowl.

Start: At the parking lot near the playground at the park's main campground
Elevation gain: 1,539 to 1,566 feet
Distance: 3.2-mile loop
Difficulty: Easy
Hiking time: 1 to 2 hours
Seasons: Best spring through fall
Fees and permits: Park entrance fee
Trail contact: Lake Louise Recreation Area, 35250 191st St., Miller, SD 57362; (605) 853-2533; https://gfp.sd.gov/parks/

Dog-friendly: Dogs must be on leash or under immediate control
Trail surface/conditions: Mowed grass
Land status: Lake Louise State Recreation Area
Nearest town(s): Miller
Other trail users: Hikers only
Maps: State park map
Trailhead amenities: Available throughout park
Maximum grade: Negligible

Pelican hanging out on Lake Louise

SHANNON TRAIL TO SCENIC OVERLOOK

A short walk to a scenic overlook at Snake Creek Recreation Area on the Missouri River. This short hike begins and ends at the day-use area near the swim beach. If wanting to hike longer, the trail also connects to the north campground.

Start: At the day-use area parking lot near the swim beach; look for "Shannon Trail" sign
Elevation gain: 1,382 to 1,428 feet
Distance: 0.6 mile out and back
Difficulty: Easy
Hiking time: 15 to 30 minutes
Seasons: Best spring through fall
Fees and permits: Park entrance fee
Trail contact: Snake Creek Recreation Area, 35316 SD Hwy. 44, Platte, SD 57369; (605) 337-2587; https://gfp .sd.gov/parks/

Dog-friendly: Dogs must be on leash or under immediate control
Trail surface/conditions: Mowed grass
Land status: Snake Creek State Recreation Area
Nearest town(s): Platte
Other trail users: Mountain bikers
Maps: State park map
Trailhead amenities: Available throughout park
Maximum grade: Negligible

View of the Missouri River from the Shannon Trail

PRAIRIE FALCON TRAIL

A prairie walk along the banks of the Missouri River at Indian Creek Recreation Area near the city of Mobridge. The Prairie Falcon Trail also connects to the Turkey Run and Orchard Oriole Trails within the park.

Start: On the eastern side of the park near picnic shelter #1
Elevation gain: 1,620 to 1,717 feet
Distance: 0.75-mile loop
Difficulty: Moderate
Hiking time: 30 minutes to 1 hour
Seasons: Best spring through fall
Fees and permits: Park entrance fee
Trail contact: Indian Creek Recreation Area, 12905 288th Ave., Mobridge, SD 57601; (605) 845-7112; https://gfp .sd.gov/parks/

Dog-friendly: Dogs must be on leash or under immediate control
Trail surface/conditions: Mowed grass
Land status: Indian Creek State Recreation Area
Nearest town(s): Mobridge
Other trail users: Mountain bikers
Maps: State park map
Trailhead amenities: Available throughout park
Maximum grade: Negligible

Prairie Falcon Trail

FOSSIL EXHIBIT TRAIL

A short, accessible loop at Badlands National Park, with exhibits of area fossils. The trail was designated a National Recreation Trail in 1980.

Start: At the trailhead 5 miles west of the Ben Reifel Visitor Center
Elevation gain: 2,663 to 2,639 feet
Distance: 0.2-mile loop
Difficulty: Easy
Hiking time: About 30 minutes
Seasons: Spring through fall
Fees and permits: Park entrance fee
Trail contact: Badlands National Park, 25216 Ben Reifel Rd., Interior, SD 57750; (605) 433-5361; www.nps.gov/badl

Dog-friendly: Dogs not allowed
Trail surface/conditions: Boardwalk
Land status: Badlands National Park
Nearest town(s): Wall, Interior
Other trail users: Hikers only
Maps: National Geographic/Trails Illustrated Topo Map No. 239; Badlands National Park brochure
Trailhead amenities: Vault toilets
Maximum grade: Negligible

Fossil Exhibit Trail

MOUNT ROOSEVELT (FRIENDSHIP TOWER)

An easy hike to Friendship Tower near the town of Deadwood, offering great views of the northern Black Hills.

Start: At the Mount Roosevelt Picnic Area in the northern Black Hills
Elevation gain: 5,535 to 5,694 feet
Distance: 0.7-mile lollipop
Difficulty: Easy
Hiking time: 30 minutes to 1 hour
Seasons: Best late spring through early fall
Fees and permits: No fees or permits required
Trail contact: Northern Hills Ranger District, 2014 N. Main St., Spearfish, SD 57783; (605) 642-4622; www.fs.usda.gov/bhnf

Dog-friendly: Leashed dogs permitted
Trail surface/conditions: Dirt path
Land status: Black Hills National Forest
Nearest town(s): Deadwood
Other trail users: Mountain bikers
Maps: Black Hills National Forest Map; BHNF Mt. Roosevelt Friendship Tower Trail No. 48; National Geographic/Trails Illustrated Topo Map No. 751
Trailhead amenities: Vault toilets, picnic tables
Maximum grade: Negligible

View of Bear Butte from Mount Roosevelt BRITTANY KAHL

STOCKADE LAKE TRAIL

A hike in Custer State Park that offers distant views of the southern Black Hills, the Needles, Black Elk Peak, and Stockade Lake. The hike has a total elevation gain of 515 feet.

Start: At the trailhead on Stockade Lake Drive, just north of the lake's swimming area in Custer State Park
Elevation gain: 5,270 to 5,653 feet
Distance: 1.5-mile lollipop
Difficulty: Strenuous to moderate
Hiking time: 40 minutes to 1.5 hours
Seasons: Best late spring through fall
Fees and permits: Park entrance fee
Trail contact: Custer State Park, 13329 US Hwy. 16A, Custer, SD 57730; (605) 255-4515; https://gfp.sd.gov/parks/

Dog-friendly: Leashed dogs permitted
Trail surface/conditions: Rocky, forested trail
Land status: Custer State Park
Nearest town(s): Custer
Other trail users: Horseback riders, mountain bikers
Maps: National Geographic/Trails Illustrated Topo Map No. 238
Trailhead amenities: Vault toilets and picnic tables nearby
Maximum grade: 12% for 0.6 mile

Icy trees along the Stockade Lake Trail

ELK MOUNTAIN NATURE TRAIL

A loop hike at the Elk Mountain Campground at Wind Cave National Park. This is one of two trails at Wind Cave National Park where dogs are allowed.

Start: At the Elk Mountain Campground, about 1 mile northwest of the park's visitor center
Elevation gain: 4,295 to 4,388 feet
Distance: 0.8-mile loop
Difficulty: Moderate then easy
Hiking time: 30 minutes to 1 hour
Seasons: Best spring through fall
Fees and permits: No fees or permits required
Trail contact: Wind Cave National Park, 26611 US Hwy. 385, Hot Springs, SD 57747; (605) 745-4600; www.nps.gov/wica

Dog-friendly: Leashed dogs permitted
Trail surface/conditions: Dirt path
Land status: Wind Cave National Park
Nearest town(s): Hot Springs
Other trail users: Hikers only
Maps: National Geographic/Trails Illustrated Topo Map No. 238; Wind Cave National Park brochure; Black Hills National Forest Map
Trailhead amenities: Toilets, picnic tables
Maximum grade: 9.7% for 0.15 mile

View from the Elk Mountain Campground area

PRAIRIE VISTA NATURE TRAIL AND NATURAL ENTRANCE

A short stroll through prairie grasslands near the Wind Cave National Park visitor center. The loop section of the trail is 0.7 mile. A paved walking path also leads to the natural entrance of Wind Cave (follow signs).

Start: At the picnic area just north of the park's visitor center
Elevation gain: 4,097 to 4,213 feet
Distance: 0.7-mile loop
Difficulty: Moderate then easy
Hiking time: 30 minutes to 1 hour
Seasons: Best spring through fall
Fees and permits: No fees or permits required
Trail contact: Wind Cave National Park, 26611 US Hwy. 385, Hot Springs, SD 57747; (605) 745-4600; www.nps.gov/wica

Dog-friendly: Leashed dogs permitted when beginning and ending at the picnic area
Trail surface/conditions: Rocky dirt path
Land status: Wind Cave National Park
Nearest town(s): Hot Springs
Other trail users: Hikers only
Maps: Geographic/Trails Illustrated Topo Map No. 238; Wind Cave National Park brochure
Trailhead amenities: Vault toilet, picnic tables
Maximum grade: 8.2% for 0.2 mile

Prairie Vista Nature Trail

COLD BROOK CANYON TRAIL

A scenic meander through a prairie valley that simultaneously explores a canyon in the southwestern section of Wind Cave National Park.

Start: At the trailhead 2 miles south of the visitor center on US 385, on the right (west) side of the road
Elevation gain: 4,152 to 4,270 feet
Distance: 2.7 miles out and back
Difficulty: Easy
Hiking time: 1 to 2 hours
Seasons: Best late spring through fall
Fees and permits: No fees or permits required
Trail contact: Wind Cave National Park, 26611 US Hwy. 385, Hot Springs, SD 57747; (605) 745-4600; www.nps.gov/wica
Dog-friendly: Dogs not allowed

Trail surface/conditions: Dirt path; limited shade
Land status: Wind Cave National Park
Nearest town(s): Hot Springs
Other trail users: Hikers only
Maps: National Geographic/Trails Illustrated Topo Map No. 238; Wind Cave National Park brochure; Black Hills National Forest Map
Trailhead amenities: None; available at nearby visitor center
Maximum grade: 8.9% for 0.25 mile (final 0.25 mile up the hill to the trailhead on return trip)

Prairie dog along the Cold Brook Canyon Trail

APPENDIX A: SUGGESTED EQUIPMENT

The following list is intended to help ensure a more enjoyable trip, but is not meant to be a complete list.

Weather in South Dakota, especially in the Black Hills, can be unpredictable. Thunderstorms occur on a regular basis in the summer months. And if you are high on a mountain trail during a sudden shower, it can get cold very quickly.

Hiking boots should be of good quality and already broken in. If you have purchased something new for a hike (tent, backpack, boots, etc.), it is a good idea to try it out, break it in, or set it up before embarking on your trek.

The following checklists will help you pack well for any day or backpack trip in South Dakota:

CLOTHING

_____ good-quality rain gear

_____ warm jacket

_____ windbreaker

_____ wind pants

_____ long underwear

_____ hiking pants

_____ lightweight long-sleeved shirt(s)

_____ T-shirts and shorts

_____ sweater or heavy shirt

_____ socks for each day plus one extra set

_____ undergarments

_____ hats—one wool, one with a sun visor

_____ gloves

_____ belt

_____ good hiking boots

_____ extra shoes or sandals for camp and stream crossings

FOOD

____ hot and cold drink mixes (tea, coffee)

____ dry food (dry your own or buy commercial meals, rice, beans, noodles)

____ hot cereal to mix with water

____ trail mix

____ high-energy snacks

HIKING EQUIPMENT

____ tent and rain fly

____ warm sleeping bag and pad with stuff sacks

____ full-size backpack

____ day pack for shorter side trips from a base camp

____ backpack stove and fuel

____ cooking pot

____ cup

____ bowl

____ utensils

____ water bottle

____ waterproof matches in container

MISCELLANEOUS

____ keys

____ driver's license, credit/debit card, cash

____ compass

____ maps

____ tick and insect repellent

____ sunscreen and lip balm

____ sunglasses

____ toilet paper

____ toothbrush

____ biodegradable soap

____ small towel/washcloth

____ small backpack shovel

____ garbage sack

____ plastic sandwich bags

____ pocketknife

____ binoculars

____ water filter or purification tablets

____ first-aid kit

____ flashlight and batteries

____ fishing gear and license

____ pocket notebook and pencil

____ 50-foot length of nylon cord

____ waterproof backpack cover

____ paperback book

____ headlamp

____ extra batteries

____ portable charger

____ cell phone and/or camera

Pasqueflower

APPENDIX B:
MANAGING AGENCIES

STATEWIDE
South Dakota Game, Fish and Parks
523 E. Capitol Ave.
Pierre, SD 57501
(605) 223-7660

GLACIAL LAKES
Fort Sisseton Historic State Park
11907 434th Ave.
Lake City, SD 57247
(605) 448-5474

Hartford Beach State Park
13672 Hartford Beach Rd.
Corona, SD 57227
(605) 432-6374

Lake Herman State Park
23409 State Park Dr.
Madison, SD 57042
(605) 256-5003

Lake Louise Recreation Area
35250 191st St.
Miller, SD 57362
(605) 853-2533

Oakwood Lakes State Park
20247 Oakwood Dr.
Bruce, SD 57220
(605) 627-5441

Pickerel Lake Recreation Area
12980 446th Ave.
Grenville, SD 57239
(605) 486-4753

Sica Hollow State Park
44950 Park Rd.
Sisseton, SD 57262
(605) 448-5701

Waubay National Wildlife Refuge
44401 134A St.
Waubay, SD 57273
(605) 947-4521

SOUTHEAST
Beaver Creek Nature Area
48351 264th St.
Valley Springs, SD 57068
(605) 594-3824

Big Sioux Recreation Area
410 W. Park St.
Brandon, SD 57005
(605) 582-7243

Good Earth State Park
26924 480th Ave.
Sioux Falls, SD 57108
(605) 213-1036

Palisades State Park
25491 485th Ave.
Garretson, SD 57030
(605) 594-3824

Newton Hills State Park
28767 482nd Ave.
Canton, SD 57013
(605) 987-2263

Union Grove State Park
30828 471st Ave.
Beresford, SD 57004
(605) 987-2263

MISSOURI RIVER

Adams Homestead and Nature Preserve
272 Westshore Dr.
McCook Lake, SD 57049
(605) 232-0873

Lewis and Clark Recreation Area
43349 SD Hwy. 52
Yankton, SD 57078
(605) 668-2985

Clay County Park
460th Ave.
Vermillion, SD 57069
(605) 659-0050

Missouri National Recreational River
508 E. 2nd St.
Yankton, SD 57078
(605) 665-0209

Farm Island Recreation Area
1301 Farm Island Rd.
Pierre, SD 57501
(605) 773-2885

Oahe Downstream Recreation Area
20439 Marina Loop Rd.
Fort Pierre, SD 57532
(605) 223-7722

Fort Pierre National Grassland
Fort Pierre Ranger District
1020 N. Deadwood St.
Fort Pierre, SD 57532
(605) 224-5517

Pease Creek Recreation Area
37270 293rd St.
Geddes, SD 57342
(605) 487-7046

Indian Creek Recreation Area
12905 288th Ave.
Mobridge, SD 57601
(605) 845-7112

Snake Creek Recreation Area
35316 SD Hwy. 44
Platte, SD 57369
(605) 337-2587

LaFramboise Island Nature Area (managed by Farm Island)
1301 Farm Island Rd.
Pierre, SD 57501
(605) 773-2885

Spirit Mound Historic Prairie
31148 SD Hwy. 19
Vermillion, SD 57069
(605) 987-2263

West Whitlock Recreation Area
16157 W. Whitlock, Ste. A
Gettysburg, SD 57442
(605) 765-9410

BADLANDS

Badlands National Park
25216 Ben Reifel Rd.
Interior, SD 57750
(605) 433-5361

Buffalo Gap National Grassland
Wall Ranger District
710 Main St.
PO Box 425
Wall, SD 57790
(605) 279-2126

Minuteman Missile National Historic Site
24545 Cottonwood Rd.
Philip, SD 57567
(605) 433-5552

National Grasslands Visitor Center
708 Main St.
PO Box 425
Wall, SD 57790
(605) 279-2125

BLACK HILLS

Black Hills National Forest
Supervisor's Office
1019 N. 5th St.
Custer, SD 57730
(605) 673-9200

Pactola Visitor Center
22995 Hwy. 385
Rapid City, SD 57702
(605) 343-8755

Bearlodge Ranger District
101 S. 21st St.
PO Box 680
Sundance, WY 82729
(307) 283-1361

Hell Canyon Ranger District
Newcastle Office
1225 Washington
Newcastle, WY 82701
(307) 746-2782

Custer Office
1019 N. 5th St.
Custer, SD 57730
(605) 673-9200

Mystic Ranger District
8221 Mount Rushmore Rd.
Rapid City, SD 57702
(605) 343-1567

Northern Hills Ranger District
2014 N. Main St.
Spearfish, SD 57783
(605) 642-4622

OTHER BLACK HILLS PUBLIC LANDS AGENCIES AND ASSOCIATIONS

Bear Butte State Park
PO Box 688
Sturgis, SD 57785
(605) 347-5240

Black Hills Trails Office
(George S. Mickelson Trail)
11361 Nevada Gulch Rd.
Lead, SD 57754
(605) 584-3896

Buffalo Gap National Grassland
Fall River Ranger District
1801 Hwy. 18 Truck Bypass
Hot Springs, SD 57747
(605) 745-4107

Bureau of Land Management South Dakota Field Office
309 Bonanza St.
Belle Fourche, SD 57717
(605) 892-7000

Bureau of Land Management Newcastle Field Office
1101 Washington
Newcastle, WY 82701
(307) 746-6600

Custer State Park
13329 US Hwy. 16A
Custer, SD 57730
(605) 255-4515

Forest Recreation Management
PO Box 1168
Hill City, SD 57745
(605) 574-4402

Jewel Cave National Monument
11149 US Hwy. 16, Bldg. B12
Custer, SD 57730
(605) 673-8300

Mount Rushmore National Memorial
13000 Hwy. 244, Bldg. 31, Ste. 1
Keystone, SD 57751
(605) 574-2523

Wind Cave National Park
26611 US Hwy. 385
Hot Springs, SD 57747
(605) 745-4600

NORTHWEST

Custer Gallatin National Forest
Sioux Ranger District
101 SE First St.
PO Box 37
Camp Crook, SD 57724
(605) 797-4432

Grand River National Grassland
Grand River Ranger District
1005 5th Ave. W.
Lemmon, SD 57638
(605) 374-3592

OTHER

South Dakota Department of Tourism
711 E. Wells Ave.
Pierre, SD 57501
(605) 773-3301

Bighorn sheep in the northern Black Hills ERIN BRADY

APPENDIX C: SELECTED BIBLIOGRAPHY AND FURTHER READING

Benton, Rachel C., Emmett Evanoff, Hugh Gregory McDonald, and Dennis O. Terry. *The White River Badlands: Geology and Paleontology* (Bloomington: Indiana University Press, 2015).

Conn, Herb and Jan. *The Jewel Cave Adventure* (Huntsville, AL: National Speleological Society, 2019).

Costello, Damian. *Black Elk: Colonialism and Lakota Catholicism* (Maryknoll, NY: Orbis Books, 2005).

DeVoto, Bernard, ed. *The Journals of Lewis and Clark* (New York: Houghton Mifflin Harcourt, 1981).

Eastman, Charles A. *The Soul of the Indian: An Interpretation* (Lincoln: University of Nebraska Press, 2020).

Froiland, Sven G. *Natural History of the Black Hills and Badlands* (Sioux Falls, SD: Center for Western Studies, 1990).

Gries, John Paul. *Roadside Geology of South Dakota* (Missoula: Mountain Press, 1996).

Hedren, Paul. *After Custer: Loss and Transformation in Sioux Country* (Norman: University of Oklahoma Press, 2011).

Horsted, Paul. *Black Hills Yesterday & Today* (Custer, SD: Golden Valley Press, 2006).

Jensen, Richard E., R. Eli Paul, and John E. Carter. *Eyewitness at Wounded Knee* (Lincoln: University of Nebraska Press, 2011).

Johnson, James R., and Gary E. Larson. *Grassland Plants of South Dakota and the Northern Great Plains* (Brookings, SD: SDSU Extension, 2016).

Johnson, W. Carter, and Dennis H. Knight. *Ecology of Dakota Landscapes: Past, Present, and Future* (New Haven, CT: Yale University Press, 2022).

Larson, Gary E. *Plants of the Black Hills and Bear Lodge Mountains* (Brookings: South Dakota State University Press, 1999).

Lauck, Jon K, ed. *Heartland River: A Cultural and Environmental History of the Big Sioux River* (Sioux Falls SD: The Center for Western Studies at Augustana University, 2022.

Lufkin, John L. *Guidebook to Geology of the Black Hills, South Dakota* (Golden, CO: Golden Publishers, 2021).

Marshall III, Joseph M. *The Lakota Way: Stories and Lessons for Living* (New York: Penguin Group, 2002).

Martin, Joel W. *The Land Looks After Us: A History of Native American Religion* (New York: Oxford University Press, 2001).

Neihardt, John. *Black Elk Speaks* (Lincoln: University of Nebraska Press, 2014).

Ostler, Jeffrey. *The Lakotas and the Black Hills: The Struggle for Sacred Ground* (New York: Penguin, 2010).

Palmer, Arthur N., Mike Wiles, Andreas Pflitsch, Hazel Barton, and Olivia Hershey. *Jewel Cave: No End in Sight* (Hot Springs, SD: Black Hills Parks and Forests Association, 2022).

Sanders, Peggy. *Wind Cave National Park: The First 100 Years* (Chicago: Arcadia Publishing, 2003).

Sandoz, Mari. *Crazy Horse: The Strange Man of the Oglalas* (Lincoln: University of Nebraska Press, 2008).

Tekiela, Stan. *Birds of the Dakotas Field Guide* (Cambridge, MN: Adventure Publishing, 2022).

Thompson, Harry F., ed. *A New South Dakota History* (Sioux Falls, SD: The Center for Western Studies at Augustana University, 2009).

Sunset at Deerfield Lake in the Black Hills

THE TEN ESSENTIALS OF HIKING

American Hiking Society

American Hiking Society recommends you pack the "Ten Essentials" every time you head out for a hike. Whether you plan to be gone for a couple of hours or several months, make sure to pack these items. Become familiar with these items and know how to use them. Learn more at **AmericanHiking.org/hiking-resources.**

1. **Appropriate Footwear**

6. **Safety Items** (light, fire, and a whistle)

2. **Navigation**

7. **First Aid Kit**

3. **Water** (and a way to purify it)

8. **Knife or Multi-Tool**

4. **Food**

9. **Sun Protection**

5. **Rain Gear & Dry-Fast Layers**

10. **Shelter**